What business leaders say about
The Art and Science of Building Customer Trust

"David's conversational style makes the topic of building customer trust come alive. This book is a must read for anyone in a business building role, grab a copy and start reading now, it will not disappoint."
Cos Rullo,
Head of Network Sales, ANZ Wealth

"If you want to get ahead of your competitors and build better relationships with your potential and existing customers, this is a must-read book."
Craig Stamp,
Executive General Manager, Device Technologies

"Trust is the foundation of any profession, it's no different for financial advice businesses. David's book is a blueprint on how to earn, build, improve and maintain professional and profitable client relationships."
Neil MacDonald,
CEO, AMP Financial Planners Association Ltd

"David has the rare skill of collecting the knowledge and wisdom from research and distilling core messages into an easily understood framework of action. You will enjoy the simplicity of how David conveys complex concepts and you will be enriched by his genuine belief that we all benefit from the formation of trusted relationships. It is a great read."

Chris Campbell,
CEO The Junction Works

"Most of us get the importance of trust in our professional and personal lives, but perhaps we underestimate the impact it has on everything around us. This book is a timely reminder for anyone to never take trust for granted."

Nicolette Barnard,
Head of Human Resources, Siemens Australia

"In *The Art and Science of Building Customer Trust*, David highlights that building trust is a prerequisite for true success in both our professional and personal lives. That's a pretty good reason to read this book."

David Stock,
Head of Learning, Wolters Kluwer

The Art and Science of Building Customer Trust

by David Penglase

Contents

1

Why trust is the new currency of business success

PUT SIMPLY, trust matters!

Trust matters because relationships matter. In your professional and personal life, almost every measure of success you have will be impacted in some way by the level of trust you earn, build and maintain.

In this increasingly competitive world, customers have more choice from where and from whom they can seek and buy their products, services or professional advice.

We very much live in a world of competitive parity. What this means is, because of increased local, national and international competition, both online and offline, any company's products, service or advice can pretty much be reproduced and offered at around the same cost and at the same level of quality, with very similar features, benefits and value.

This makes it tough to compete, differentiate and to stand out in a world of sameness.

As you read through these pages, you'll learn how applying the principles and strategies from *The Art and Science of Building Customer Trust* will help you:

- differentiate from your competitors
- earn more new, repeat and referral business
- increase your sense of pride and engagement in your business
- gain more clarity on how to find, win and keep customers, and
- fast-track the success you seek in your business goals.

The Art and Science of Building Customer Trust is based on having a genuine intention to understand what a customer wants or needs, and to deliver the best product, advice, service or solution to match those wants or needs.

Whether you're a business owner, team leader, salesperson, customer service specialist or professional adviser, whether you've had years of experience or are just starting out in business, I'm confident you will gain value from this book.

When you think about it, regardless of the industry or profession, business is about finding, winning and keeping customers. Sure, there are other important things that are going on (manufacturing, warehousing, distribution, research and development, people management, etc.), but if these other functions aren't geared toward helping find, win and keep customers, you end up with an internally focused business culture, rather than a culture focused on Building Customer Trust.

What I'm suggesting is that every person in every role ought to be positively impacting finding, winning or keeping customers. This is a book about winning new, repeat and referral business through the sales and service roles. You will notice I combine and use *sales and service people* throughout the book. Both sales and customer service roles impact the finding, winning and keeping of clients.

My choice of using the combined roles is to represent and include the broader roles of customer service, professional advice, sales and business development.

If you're a professional adviser, and don't think of yourself as being in a sales or customer service role, let me suggest that you don't 'give' advice ... customers pay for it (and therefore you're selling it). When you provide customers with advice on which product (financial, legal, medical, etc.) you believe they should select to achieve their goals, wants or needs, your aim is that they buy the product. In other words, you're selling it.

However, if you're still a bit concerned about the idea of selling, based on your own experiences with some pushy or unethical salespeople, you'll find the *Art and Science of Building Customer Trust* is not only based on ethical communication and business practice, it is also well supported by evidence-based behavioural science and positive psychology research.

Yet while there is significant scientific research within the Building Customer Trust process, I am convinced there is also a subtle art form in the way we communicate as humans. This book will share both the art and science of Building Customer Trust.

Let me position this by getting you to use your imagination for a moment to explore what might be possible in a business world based on trust.

Imagine this ...

Imagine a world where *every* customer had access to the latest mobile device app, which they could use to detect whether a sales or service person was telling the truth?

Imagine if, when using this new app, a customer could detect what was really motivating a sales or service person to recommend a product or service.

If it was real, this app might be called the *Intention-Ometer App* (or IOA because we live in a world where Three Letter Acronyms (TLAs) seem to be the norm). This IOA would measure the truth about what was motivating a sales or service person's approach and recommendations.

If this IOA was real, it would revolutionise the confidence of customers and would fast-track their buying decisions. Put simply, they would buy more confidently and buy more often.

Armed with their IOA, every customer would be able to avoid making poor buying decisions by exposing any sales or service person who tried to lie, distort the truth, or who was selling and recommending a product, service or advice, based on self-interest, rather than based on the customer's best interest.

Again, what this means is, armed with their IOA, every customer would be more confident and comfortable to buy whenever their IOA confirmed they were dealing with an honest sales or service person.

If this IOA was real, it would also revolutionise the way sales and service people communicated with customers.

They would quickly realise that being honest and selling or recommending products and services with the best interest of their customers as their prime motivator *would result in them selling more.*

There would no longer be any need for tricky, manipulative communication, persuasion, selling or closing techniques ... those approaches would be quickly exposed by the IOA and result in 'no sale'.

Wait on ... just stop for a moment and think deeply about the simple logic of this imaginary scenario.

If customers would buy more and sales and service people would sell more in a world where the honesty and trustworthiness of the sales or service person was revealed, doesn't it just make sense that

What if every customer knew what you were thinking ... what if they knew the intentions behind your actions?

sales and service people in the real world, right now, ought to be selling and making their product or service recommendations based on honesty, trustworthiness and in the client's best interest?

Now, you might be tempted to think this is all a bit soft and too far removed from the reality of the cut and thrust of business.

However, what we know from an increasing amount of scientific research is that we humans are encoded to respond positively to trustworthiness and honesty[1], and if business owners, leaders and their sales and service teams ignore this or undervalue its importance, they will, quite frankly, be undermining their own success.

Aside from the scientific evidence, just stop and think about the type of sales or service person you'd personally like to buy from.

Wouldn't you like to buy from someone you knew was not only an expert on whatever product or service they were offering, but importantly, that you could also trust they had your best interest at top of mind in recommending any product or service to you?

I'm *not saying* all you need to be successful in business is to be honest and trustworthy. In fact, you might very well be honest and trustworthy, but if you lack the competence or knowledge to effectively communicate with customers in ways that demonstrate the reasons why they ought to buy your products and services, the result is still a lack of trust ... and 'no sale'.

Your success in business is also influenced by a host of other factors, including the need to have a product, service or advice that customers want to buy; the necessity for your products, services or advice to be priced competitively; the need to have some point of differentiation that is meaningful for customers to be able to determine whether to buy from you or from your competitor (other than just on price alone); and the loyalty that customers often place with their preferred brands or suppliers.

A reality check

Almost every business across every industry or profession will at some time have issues with the quality, pricing, terms or delivery of their product, service or advice process. Sometimes one or more of these issues will make it more difficult to sell, even when the sales or service person genuinely believes their product, service or advice will help their customers.

What I'm highlighting here is, there isn't a panacea or single 'secret' to winning more new, repeat and referral customers. If that's what you're looking for you're going to be disappointed, and you're going to get very tired and confused by chasing the next 'big thing' in how to deliver exceptional buying experiences for your customers.

And just thinking positively isn't the answer!

Positive thinking might be the mainstay of the world of self-help, and while it's a good place to start, you're going to need a heck of a lot more than positive thinking and optimism to succeed in the disruptive and competitive world of business in the 21st century.

In fact, what we know from a range of positive psychology research is that, at times, positive thinking and being overly optimistic can have negative outcomes.[2] Relying on hope or optimism without taking measured and intentional action, and without adjusting your activities when your results aren't what you want or need, is quite simply a recipe for failure.

Beware of chasing non-evidence-based self-help hyperbole.

Many people across the globe received a reality slap after being sucked into the flawed thinking of simply relying on what is touted as *the law of attraction*. Hopefully you missed or ignored this self-help nonsense, which can be loosely described as *believing if you want something enough it will manifest itself into your life*.

Sure, wanting more new, repeat and referral customers (or anything else for that matter) might be a good place to start, but just thinking about getting rich or just thinking (and hoping) about being successful in business or succeeding in any other area of your life isn't enough. You need to take action!

The Art and Science of Building Customer Trust provides you with an evidence-based blueprint that combines the mindset and actions you need to be more successful in winning more new, repeat and referral business. And it's all about trust.

The Triangle of Three Trusts

I'm confident you already 'get' that trust is important. Most people do. But let's dig a little more deeply into what it means to trust and to be trusted.

The Triangle of Three Trusts helps to explain that trust consists of self-trust (the *confidence* you have to trust in yourself); trust in others (the *courage* to trust others); and earning others' trust (having the combined *character and competence* to be trusted by others).

Let's start with the confidence required for self-trust.

Self-trust

At the pointy end of the inverted Triangle of Three Trusts is self-trust. I've purposefully inverted the triangle to have you visualise if you don't have self-trust, your capacity to trust others and to earn others' trust would quickly become unbalanced.

So, before you can have the courage to trust in others, and to earn others' trust, you need to have self-trust.

When you think about it, your future self needs to trust your current self.

I know that's a bit of a weird way to think about self-trust ... but stay with me on this for a moment.

If your current self (in other words, you, right now) isn't making positive choices and taking positive action to flourish, both professionally and personally, your future self is going to be negatively impacted.

If instead of an apple a day, you've decided on a burger and fries a day, it won't take long for you to put on weight and potentially experience some poor health.

If instead of pursuing opportunities to learn and grow, you make the decision that you don't need to learn anything new, your future self is going to find it tough to keep up with a constantly changing and disruptive world where others are continually learning and growing.

Self-trust is about striving for your personal best. I know it's a bit of a glib statement, but it's also pretty hard to dismiss as anything other than a good idea. To continually try to be a better communicator, better colleague, better service provider, better team member, better person in your personal and professional life isn't always easy – but your future self will be so thankful when looking back over the years at your positive choices, decisions, actions and results.

To help you set some goals around self-trust, ask yourself this: What am I *not* doing today that, if I did it, would help me be an even better version of me in my professional and personal life?

This is not about perfection – perfectionism is zero-sum game. I reckon *betterism* is a more achievable goal. Strive for continual improvement.

The relationship you have with yourself forms the pointy end of the Triangle of Three Trusts because if you can't trust yourself, it's going to be hard for you to trust in others, and even harder to earn the trust of others.

Trust others

Beyond self-trust is the courage you need to trust others.

For you to be able to deliver exceptional customer experiences, at times you will need to have the courage to place your trust in other people.

However, there is an important difference between having *blind faith* in trusting someone, and having *realistic accountable trust* in others.

Blind faith relies on hope, whereas realistic accountable trust involves contingency planning, constant communication, and reinforcement of consequences. That kind of courage requires a commitment to taking the personal responsibility to manage the trust you are placing in others.

Now let's consider the combined character and competence you'll need to earn the trust of others – especially your customers.

Earn others' trust

Earning others' trust means promising what you can deliver and delivering on your promises.

It's important to realise that your customers (and others in your professional and personal life) will judge your trustworthiness not only on your level of competence or capacity to do what you say you can do. They also judge it on your character – the way you go about doing what you say you will do.

As I've mentioned previously, for most of my adult life I've been academically and experientially researching what causes people to think, feel and act the way they do, and what causes relationships in our personal and professional lives to flourish.

When thinking about earning the trust of others, I particularly like this quote from Aristotle: *"Our actions and behaviours are our morals shown in conduct"*. When I first read that quote I had just become a father for the first time and the words leaped off the page at me.

Without wanting to overly dramatise what happened, it was in that instant I realised that my son would look at my actions and behaviour – what I said and what I did – and he would be seeing my morals and values on display.

I made the decision there and then to be more consciously aware of my role as a father and demonstrate morals and values I would be proud of – not only for myself, but also for my son.

We now have two adult sons and while, like all of us, along the way I've made mistakes and sometimes haven't been the 'perfect role model', the words of Aristotle are always at top of my mind and driving my choices and actions.

I share this with you because while this book is about The Art and Science of Building Customer Trust, the reality is: trust will impact almost every measure of success in your personal as well as your professional life.

Aristotle is suggesting, advising and perhaps even warning us that everything we say and do sends loud and clear messages to the world about who we are and what we stand for. In other words, *your actions and your behaviours put your character on display*.

Here's another way to think about this: *People Get Your Truth!* Over time, your intentions, promises, actions and results will either promote you as being trustworthy or expose you as being untrustworthy.

Clients will quickly determine your truth, based on their perceptions of your intentions, promises, actions and results.

The internet has set information free ... just knowing stuff about your products and services isn't all that helpful in sales and delivering exceptional customer service.

If you don't have a positive intention for your customers (an intention to only recommend, advise and sell customers something that is in their best interest and will improve their life in some way), then your intention is more likely to be self-interest (personal or organisational), and customers will pick up on that truth.

The result ... at worst, no sale or, in the very least, reduced sales success.

In the pages that follow, I will provide you with scientific evidence that validates why it's important for you to develop a sense of clarity and intrinsic belief in your intention for your customers – what you want *for* them, not what you want *from* them.

When you develop this sense of clarity and belief in your intention for your customers, you will be able to fast-track the trust-building process essential to long-term sales success and for delivering exceptional customer experiences.

Adopting this philosophy in practice is important, because there's been a major shift in the psychology of buying that many leaders and their sales and service people have missed.

A big shift in the psychology of buying

We live in a world of constant change and across most, if not all, business and professional sectors, increased competition is making it more difficult for sales and service people to differentiate their products and services, whether that's by features, benefits, quality or price.

Your customers now have potentially more capacity and choice to find what they're after than ever before. The internet has created a massive change in the psychology of buying.

In his best-selling book, FREE[3], Chris Anderson highlights that information is now free. The majority of people in the world have access to masses of technical information, pictures, videos and other customers' feedback and opinions about products and services they're interested in. The internet allows people to access almost any information about almost any product or service from anywhere.

This has caused a major shift in the way people buy today ... a major shift in the psychology of buying.

Whether you're in business-to-business or business-to-consumer sales, regardless of whether they're buying products, services or professional advice, in addition to being able to buy both on and/or off line, it's the customers' decision-making process that's changed.

It's this new psychology of buying that you need to be aware of and that your sales, service and customer engagement process needs to be aligned with. Otherwise, you're putting your success at risk.

I will expand on what's changed in the customers' decision-making process more specifically in a moment, but for now what I want to highlight is that this change has created a problem for many sales and service people who place high importance on their product and service knowledge.

I'm not saying that having a high level of product and service knowledge isn't important – of course it is. However, buyers now have a minimum level of expectation that sales and service people will have expert knowledge in the products and services they provide.

Why? Because as I've just highlighted, the consumer now has access to just as much information about products and services as the sales and service people they're potentially going to be buying from.

The devaluing of your product knowledge

This has created a new base level for sales and service people: consumers now won't place as much value on (or feel they should pay for) being just provided with information about the product or service they're after. They won't see the provision of information about products and services as something of value – because they can access that information themselves from the internet.

While consumers may not be willing to pay for information, they will value and pay for advice.

However, all is not lost. While consumers may not be willing to value or pay for information, they will certainly value and pay for advice.

Even when people really want or need a product, service or professional advice, with so much information available on so many sites, they can become overwhelmed, which overloads their decision-making capacity and paralyses them into procrastination.

What they need is:

- someone who will provide them with professional advice to sort through the information and on what choices they ought to make for their personal and specific situation
- someone who will help them break free of their inertia, confusion and feeling of being overwhelmed
- someone who has and demonstrates a clear and genuine intention to provide a product, service or advice that is in the client's best interest
- someone who they can trust.

This book will help you better understand this shift in the psychology of buying, and help you to become that *intentional trusted adviser* that customers and clients today are seeking. And when you implement the process outlined in this book, you will be able to proudly provide the best possible buying experience for your customers, and in so doing, increase your capacity to win more new, repeat and referral business.

This is a book about Building Customer Trust. I'd like to take a moment to explore in a little more detail what it means to trust and to be trusted.

When we take trust for granted

Most of us get that trust is important in our personal and professional lives. We don't have to search very hard for examples of where trust has been fractured or broken. My good friend and author of *The Truth About Trust*, Vanessa Hall[4], expresses this beautifully by saying, "Trust is fragile".

Research from the Edelman Group[5] and The World Economic Forum[6] suggests that trust across a range of industries and professions is at risk. This has serious economic and personal implications. In his best-selling book, *The Speed of Trust*, Stephen Covey[7] reports on research that suggests trust impacts almost every measure of success in an organisation.

OK, so we get that trust is important, but here's the real problem. Even when we 'get' that something is important, it is natural for humans to just take things for granted ... even the important things.

When we take things for granted we devalue them ... while they're still important to us, we just get used to them, and this results in us unintentionally (mindlessly) devaluing the very thing that is of value to us.

How quickly do people get used to a beautiful view they see every day from their home or office window and take it for granted? The same can happen with a new car. It quickly loses its newness and we take it for granted. Sadly, we get used to new things very quickly. This is true of any relationship we might have as well. When we unintentionally just get used to the other person in a relationship, when we take them for granted, we devalue the relationship and this puts it at risk.

This is also true for trust. When we take trust for granted, we devalue it. As I've mentioned earlier, most of us get that trust is important, and in business we get that trust is the foundation upon which most sales, if not all, are made.

However, in the disruptive and competitive world that many sales and service people operate in, it is very easy to just take trust for granted ... and this puts trust at risk. When trust is at risk in a buyer-seller relationship, our capacity to win more new, repeat and referral sales is at risk as well.

This book will help you put trust at the centre of your focus – where it ought to be. You see, you don't *get* trust ... you earn it. And there's a real danger that if you're unintentionally just accepting that trust is important, but not consciously, mindfully, intentionally and practically focused on a process that helps you to earn trust, you may be in fact unintentionally disengaging from the very thing that is the foundation of every professional (and personal) relationship you have.

In a world where your clients are suffering from information overload, and are influenced by what we know is an increasing level of distrust, they need sales and service people who they can trust to provide advice that creates a clear path for them to make wise, comfortable and confident buying decisions. They don't have the mythical *Intention-Ometer App*, so they need and want to buy from sales and service people they can rely on and trust.

Success in business, sales and customer service of course requires many things. You'll need to develop a mastery level of product, service, technical or compliance knowledge; to balance the tasks of finding, winning and retaining clients; to manage the ever-increasing 'paperwork' or administrative reporting and updating of CRM (customer relationship management) systems; to have a client engagement process in place that is aligned with the new way that buyers want to buy; to have a process that helps you earn the trust of your clients; to develop proactive rather than reactive resilience when things don't go your way (because they won't always go your way); and I'm sure you'll be able to think of a number of other elements that will contribute to your long-term success.

In this first chapter you've learned about the various forms of trust in your life – the confidence required for self-trust; the courage required to trust in others; and the combined character and competence to earn others' trust. We've also explored why you need a process to hold yourself accountable to earn, build and maintain customer trust.

In the pages that follow you'll be introduced to a practical and easy-to-implement, six-step, self-coaching process specifically designed to help you earn, build and maintain customer trust: The Building Customer Trust process.

In chapter two we'll define what it really means to build customer trust and explore three buyer exit ramps that you'll need to proactively manage to win more new, repeat and referral business.

In chapter three you'll gain a deeper understanding about what science tells us about the mindset of success. You'll learn about what the latest research is telling us about what drives your motivation and what you can do to tap into those drivers when you need them most.

In chapter four you'll be introduced to the Building Customer Trust process, which is a six-step blueprint you'll be able to immediately implement with positive results. You'll develop more clarity around the psychology of building customer trust and learn a very powerful, evidence-based and yet very practical way to create a buying environment where your customers feel more comfortable, confident and trusting to buy from you.

In chapter five you'll explore the power of value-discovery questions. These are questions you will craft and ask your customers, that will have the capacity to positively shift the way your customers think about the value they can gain when buying from you. When you ask value-discovery questions you help your customers gain clarity about what's most important about the product, service or advice they are seeking, and enable you to help them prioritise what's most important. You'll discover why asking value-discovery questions (without the need to turn the communication into an interrogation) will fast-track the trust-building process between you and your customers.

In chapter six you'll discover how to take the important information your customers have provided you with through answering your value-discovery questions and present your product, service or advice the customer is seeking in a tailored and personalised way that distances you from your competitors and engages the customer in ways that will make them feel comfortable and confident to proceed and buy from you.

In chapter seven you'll be presented with the challenging truth that the majority of obstacles and objections customers typically raise when being presented with a recommended product, service or advice are mostly the fault of the sales or customer service person. What you'll discover is the more typical and traditional reactive way of handling buyer obstacles and objections is flawed, and what you can do to more proactively discover, manage and overcome any potential buyer obstacle or objection.

In chapter eight you'll discover why the traditional end-goal of closing the sale is also a flawed approach to building customer trust and winning more new, repeat and referral customers. Professional sales and service providers don't close sales; they also don't ask the customer if they'd like to buy. They make clear, confident and value-focused recommendations of the next appropriate steps for the customer to receive and achieve the value they are seeking.

In chapter nine you'll explore just how well you are reinforcing, validating and rewarding your customers' decisions to buy from you. This is the advocacy- and loyalty-building step in the Building Customer Trust process, and it is the one that many businesses fail on. In the pursuit of winning the sale, they ignore or simply don't realise the quickest way to their next sale is through post-sale strategies that make the customer want to either buy again, or to refer other potential customers to the business.

In chapter ten, I leave you with some summary points about the power of your intentions and the positive impact they have for you and your customers as you implement the Building Customer Trust process.

CHAPTER SUMMARY
> ‣ Your intentions matter
> ‣ The psychology of buying has shifted
> ‣ You don't *get* trust ... you earn it
> ‣ Consumers are suffering from information overload
> ‣ Information is not as valuable as advice

2

Defining what it really means to Build Customer Trust

WHETHER YOU'RE IN a sales or service role, take a moment before reading on to think about how you define selling ... what's involved in the sales and buying process?

Whatever words came to you, now take a moment and think about how you would define what it takes to build customer trust.

I'm wondering how similar your first and second definitions are?

Here's how I'm recommending you define the process of Building Customer Trust (which, when put into practice, will result in you winning more new, repeat and referral customers):

Building Customer Trust is a process of building intentional trust relationships, with the aim to create reciprocal value on a continual basis.

Let's take a moment to analyse this definition.

The first component is: Building Customer Trust is a *process*. Traditional sales approaches tend to be more project than process focused. They typically place a lot of pressure on the sales or service person to 'close the sale'. This becomes the end-point of the selling project, and also creates a lot of unnecessary pressure, not only on the sales or service person, but also on the customer.

The Building Customer Trust process, however, is not project or end-point focused. It is a process that has certain stages, objectives and action principles that will be outlined in this book and, when implemented, will enable you to know exactly where you and your customers are up to in that buying process.

This is important from a self-coaching point of view, as well as for sales or service leaders to be able to coach the potential of their people.

Without a process of Building Customer Trust, successful communication and customer engagement are left to chance. Without a process, planning and review of any customer communication becomes troublesome. Without a process, coaching and development of sales and service teams is more difficult. Without a process, the quality of the customer engagement can be significantly reduced.

You may be thinking, "Wait a moment – won't following a set process box me into communicating, selling or serving customers in just one structured way?" Stay with me on this one – the answer is: definitely not. Process will give you more flexibility when communicating with your customers – flexibility with focus!

Maybe you're not a structured type of person, and the thought of needing to follow a process when communicating with customers is not appealing. But here is a paradox that you might like to consider: it's called the **structure-flexibility paradox**. It simply suggests that the more structured you are, the more flexible you can be.

Following a structure or process when communicating with existing and potential customers can enable you to be more flexible with focus. What this means is that you will be able to cater for each customer situation better, because each customer will want you to communicate with them in a different way.

Building Customer Trust is a process that is flexible with focus and will help you to understand clearly what needs to be achieved to earn and win a sale and create value for a customer. How you apply the process flexibly will depend on your own personality and style.

If you've been exposed to rigid "Do this, then this; ask this, then that; say this; do that" type of selling or customer engagement approaches then you're certainly justified in any scepticism or apprehension you might have about a sales or service process.

However, Building Customer Trust is a process where you'll discover an intuitively flexible approach that enables you to be who you are, by using your own personality and values to help differentiate you in a competitive market place.

Returning to our definition of Building Customer Trust, it is a process of *building intentional trust relationships.*

The intangible glue that binds sustainable new, repeat and referral business is *trust.* Sure, the products, service or advice you sell are important; the communication strategies, the branding and your own personality also are strong contributors to your overall success in sales and delivering exceptional customer experiences.

However, each of these, in one way or another, adds to (or detracts from) the level of trust that potential and existing customers have in their relationship with you.

The sameness syndrome in sales and service

Sales and service people work in a competitive world where the sameness syndrome abounds. The sameness syndrome has been created because in a competitive world products and services are quickly replicated, produced and offered with the same quality, and at the same price. What this means is, especially when there is no real point of difference in quality or price in the mind of the customer, it is often the strength of the trusted relationship that causes a buyer to choose one sales or service person over another.

The intangible glue that binds sustainable new, repeat and referral sales is business!

However, you don't *get* trust, you earn it, and for this reason it's important to understand the psychology behind any hesitation, fears or apprehension that some customers might experience when they are purchasing more important, meaningful or valuable products or services. These are often referred to as *buyer exit ramps*.

Three buyer exit ramps

The buyer's journey is a bit like a highway, and along the highway a number of exit ramps appear and cause the buyer to hesitate and consider whether they ought to take the exit ramp or not.

Each of these ramps is formed in the customer's mind by a question they are asking themselves about what they're experiencing along their buyer's journey. The more important the purchase, the more likely it is that the customer feels higher levels of apprehension, or even fear, during certain stages of the buying experience.

Now, when I refer to these exit ramps appearing in the customer's mind, I'm referring to questions that they ask silently to themselves, and their 'inner voice' starts a conversation that becomes louder and more consciously evident to the customer ... but they may never verbalise the fear, apprehension or question that they're asking themselves.

Each of these buyer exit ramps that appear in the customers' minds are really thoughts they have, questions they are asking themselves but they may never ask out loud. However, it is important that as a sales or service person you are aware they exist and you manage them as best you can. The process of Building Customer Trust will enable you to do just that.

The first exit ramp is known as the **Initial Contact Exit Ramp**. This ramp is a question that pops into the customer's mind when they start thinking about the need to make a purchase of a product, service or seek advice. It is heightened when they first meet with the sales or service person, and continues to pop into their mind along their buying journey.

What's your inner voice saying to you about your belief in the real value of your product, service and company?

Their inner voice starts to ask, "What's this buying experience going to be like?"

Here's an example of what this exit ramp can look like. I remember when I needed to buy a new car. I'd been at this car dealership for about five minutes. No one seemed to be around; then suddenly this salesperson appeared from nowhere. He startled me a little, because I hadn't seen him, and he greeted me with "G'day! How ya doing?"

"I'm fine, thanks", I replied (and I remember thinking to myself, what is this guy going to try on me?).

"I've been watching you", he said with a cheesy grin.

"Have you?" I replied (thinking very loudly inside my head now, "I don't think I like you").

"Yeah," he continued, "I've been watching how you walk, what you're wearing and how you're standing right now, and I reckon I've already worked out what sort of car you're going to buy from me today". He paused, then asked, "What do you think about that?"

Well, I thought of a few things, none of which I will put into words here, but simply said to him, "I think you should keep thinking about it, because I'm leaving". And with that, I just turned and walked away. I got to my own car that I'd parked outside the dealership and turned back to find him still standing where I had left him. He must have been thinking, "What went wrong?"

He had lived up to every negative stereotype some people still have about sales or service people. Even if he was just trying to be funny, he didn't add any value to the conversation by saying something like that. Now, maybe I was a bit too sensitive, but I took the first buyer exit ramp physically. Others may have stayed physically, but emotionally taken the exit ramp by listening to what the car salesperson had to say, already having decided not to buy from him.

There is a sub-text going on here. The first buyer exit ramp is where the customer asks themselves, "What's this buying experience going to be like?" and then, depending on what the sales or service person says or does, the sub-text goes something like this: "Is what this sales or service person saying, asking or doing of value to me? Do I get the sense that they are genuinely trying to engage and help me, or are they not really interested in me and only interested in themselves and making a sale?"

The Building Customer Trust process will help you better manage this first buyer exit ramp, which continues throughout the buyer's journey. Customers are constantly assessing their buying experience. The former CEO of Scandinavian Airlines, Jan Carlzon, referred to these moments along the buyer's journey as 'Moments of Truth'[8]. Every point of contact a customer has with your company is a moment of truth, where they are assessing their buying and customer experience.

A key business success strategy is for you to map out as many of these potential points of contact customers have with you and your business, and to determine ways to ensure each one is a positive experience for the customer.

These moments of truth include the customers' experience when visiting your website; their experience when phoning or emailing your company; their experience in-store or at your office; their experience when being greeted by a sales or service person; and their experiences throughout their buying journey.

Every business needs to manage these moments of truth by building exceptional customer experiences that remove the first buyer exit ramp.

The second buyer exit ramp is the **Decision Point Exit Ramp.** This ramp is again a question the customer silently asks themselves at the point when they start thinking about making a buying decision. They will typically like the 'offer' that's being presented to them. They're thinking to themselves, "This sounds really good ... I think I will buy this from this person". Then the second buyer exit ramp appears in the form of a three-letter word ... '*But*'. The client thinks, "But ... if I say yes ... what risk might I run ... what could go wrong ... how do I know this is the best deal I can get?"

Every moment with a customer is a moment of truth ... People Get Your Truth!

At this point the more the sales or service person tries to push for an early close, the wider the second buyer exit ramp appears. As you learn more about the process of Building Customer Trust, you'll discover ways to proactively manage this second buyer exit ramp before the 'But' word enters the customer's mind and potentially stops them from buying.

The third buyer exit ramp is the **Post-Sale Exit Ramp**, which happens, as the name suggests, after the sale. The customer has bought. They've returned to their home or office and sat for a moment and they hear themselves say, "What have I just done? Was it a good decision?" In traditional sales training this was referred to as buyer's remorse. However, this is much more than buyer's remorse, because the question the customer typically is asking at this isn't so much about was it a good decision to buy, but rather was it a good decision to buy from *you?*

Left unresolved, this question – this exit ramp – will negatively impact the potential for you to earn the advocacy of your customers and limit your potential to create customer loyalty to you, your products, services and your company. It will also, if left unaddressed, result in you limiting your opportunities for repeat and/or referral business.

Yes, trust is important and as you discover and implement the process of Building Customer Trust, you'll be positively placed to proactively manage each of these buyer exit ramps so they don't appear in your customers' minds. You'll fast-track the trust-building process and win more new, repeat and referral business.

One of the underlying principles of Building Customer Trust is to promise what you can deliver and deliver on what you promise. This is central to you being able to earn, build and maintain trust relationships with your customers.

However, this is where many of the approaches of relationship-based selling have caused confusion for many sales and service people. While relationship selling focuses on building relationships, which is positive, for many sales or service people, all this has resulted in is the building of relationships, and not necessarily the achievement of more new, repeat or referral sales.

This is where the Building Customer Trust process is different. Returning to our definition, Building Customer Trust is a process of building intentional trust relationships *with the aim to create reciprocal value* – value for customers and, in return, value for the company through the achievement of more new, repeat and referral business.

The 'soft-sell' and relationship-based selling approaches often and confusingly overemphasise the relationship and underemphasise the reality that the purpose or goal of earning and building the intentional trust relationship in the first place is (a) to certainly create value for the customer and (b) importantly, that this is done in a way that the company can make a profit – in other words, there is a recognition by both buyer and seller that the buying and selling process is about the attainment of reciprocal value.

Customers have some basic expectations. Thinking about these is fundamental to your understanding and maximising the potential to give and receive reciprocal value.

So, what do clients implicitly and explicitly expect from a buying situation?

- They expect a quality product.
- They expect a fair and competitive price.
- They expect to be treated with respect.
- They expect the product or service to perform its function well.
- They expect, should there be any problems, that they will be fixed within fair and equitable warranty and guarantee guidelines.
- They expect to be told the truth.
- They understand that businesses must make a profit, and cheapest is not always best, but they mostly want the best price possible.
- They expect a competent level of product or service knowledge.
- They expect to be given appropriate time and information to make a wise choice.

How well do you set and manage the expectations of your customers?

Central to the process of Building Customer Trust is how you gain and demonstrate your understanding of the customer's expectations, needs, wants, concerns and other elements important to their specific circumstances.

Buyers tune in very quickly to the intention and attitude of sales or service people. Let me repeat the underlying philosophy of the Building Customer Trust process, which is: *People Get Your Truth.*

So as a sales or service person, it's not only important for you to understand the buyers' expectations but to also understand what's driving your own attitude, your personal philosophy and belief about who you are, what you're selling, what you're providing, the company you work for, and the value you create when you sell what you sell, and provide the service you provide.

Each of these beliefs and expectations is brought to the buyer-seller relationship very early in the process, and they're driven by your intention, or the motivation behind your actions.

There's a big difference between someone who genuinely believes in the value they can create when they sell, and genuinely asks, "May I help you", and someone who lacks personal belief in themselves and their products, service or advice and asks the same question only because they have been told to ask it.

Again, this is all about understanding the impact of reciprocal value. You can't give value if you don't understand what value a customer seeks. And if you can't give value, it will be very rare that you receive value in return.

You will have heard the maxim, "What we give out we get back". We get the new, repeat and referral business we deserve. When we provide real value, we receive the value we deserve.

What we give out to potential and existing customers in our thoughts, attitude, words and actions sends loud and clear messages about who we are and what we represent. People want to do business with someone they can trust. They want to do business with someone who strives to understand their needs, specific to their own situation.

Through your intentions, thoughts, attitudes, words and actions you demonstrate your genuine desire to discover needs and wants that are specific to each potential and existing customer's situation. In doing so, you are demonstrating a customer-centric and value focus, and therefore increasing the confidence and comfort level of those considering whether to buy from you.

That's the power of reciprocity.

No end-point to a transaction

The final component of our definition of Building Customer Trust is that it is practised on *a continual basis*.

The Building Customer Trust process does not have an end-point. It doesn't end when the sale is made or, said another way, when the customer has bought. The delivery of value continues long after the sale. This may be through some follow-up or post-sale value being created for the buyer by the sales or service person or, because of the delivery of value and the validation of trust, it may be by way of warm referrals of friends, family or colleagues by the buyer.

Quite often, what is done after the sale will have the greatest impact on creating an advocate in the customer. Consider the athlete who enters the 100-metre sprint. As a sprinter, they don't want to stop at the 100-metre line: they would need to slow down before they got there. As a 100-metre sprinter, an athlete needs to run 105 or 110 metres. That way, they're hitting the finish line at full speed. They sprint beyond the finish.

One of the keys to successful selling and creating exceptional customer experiences is not just to make the sale and finish at the 100-metre line. This is where focusing everything on closing the sale is a flawed strategy. The traditional selling mantras of always be closing and close early, close often and close hard, have set many sales and service people up for failure.

If your focus is on 'closing the sale' you're more than likely creating exit ramps your customers will take, and this will result in 'no sale.'

Sure, you want to win the sale; but if you are focused on just closing the sale, there is the danger of not fully understanding the customer's needs and, more importantly, not delivering on those needs in ways that make the customer want to buy from you again, or recommend you and refer others to you.

In other words, it's creating a false positive if you win the sale, but lose longer-term reciprocal value.

In a world where customers now readily post and share feedback on their experiences with companies and their sales and service providers, it just makes sense that every moment with a potential or existing client is a moment of truth. It's a moment where you need to be mindfully aware of your intentions, promises and actions, and mindfully aware of the buying experience you're creating.

Again ... People Get Your Truth!

Arguably it's quite easy to get a sale. But it's what you do after the sale, and on a continual basis where appropriate, that creates extended, meaningful value for the customer. This builds stronger and more intentional trust relationships, resulting in a more positive buying experience for customers and increases the reciprocal value you receive through more new, repeat and referral clients.

I've so far introduced you to the importance of trust and you've now got an overview of the definition of the Building Customer Trust process.

Before providing you with a blueprint that will outline the specific steps, objectives and action principles of Building Customer Trust, in the next chapter we dig a little deeper into how your intentions impact your mindset and how developing your sense of self-determination can positively impact your personal and professional success.

CHAPTER SUMMARY

- ▸ Focus on the value of your advice
- ▸ Your intention for the client matters
- ▸ Building Customer Trust is not just about building relationships
- ▸ Building Customer Trust is a process, not a project
- ▸ The goal of Building Customer Trust is to create reciprocal value
- ▸ Value continuity is delivered well after a purchase

3

Getting your mindset right

I'VE ALREADY MENTIONED that simply relying on the self-help mantra of the power of positive thinking to be successful in selling just won't work. While thinking positively is of course a good place to start, positive thinking without action is simply hope or dreaming, and it's not what gets things achieved.

My dad shared with me a very simple piece of wisdom that is inescapable in its truth. Dad said, "If you want to get stuff done ... do stuff!" Thinking about it just won't get it done. I'm not saying thinking positively isn't of value. But I am saying that your success in sales and customer service will largely depend on you being mindful of what you are thinking and how that might be impacting your decisions and actions.

SAY
↓
FEEL
↓
ACT
↓
HABIT
↓
SUCCESS

The flow of the five words on the right of this page is a simple yet powerful way to explain how we greatly impact our own personal and professional success. What you say to yourself (what you think - your inner voice) will significantly impact how you feel, which will significantly impact how you act, which will over time form the basis of your habits, which will significantly impact your success in your professional and personal life.

We are constantly talking to ourselves. We have internal conversations and make silent decisions and choices based on our life experiences and personal beliefs.

In this chapter I will outline three well-researched and evidence-based approaches to better understanding how your thoughts and what you do with them can impact your success in your professional and personal life.

One way our internal thinking, feelings, actions and results are influenced is by our mindset. Stanford University psychologist Carol Dweck's research suggests that there are two distinct mindsets: *fixed mindset* and *growth mindset*.[9] If you've got a fixed mindset, you will believe that things like your intelligence and your natural talents are fixed traits that can't change. People with fixed mindsets typically believe that it is their intelligence and talents that create success, rather than the effort they put in to whatever they do. They tend to lack resilience when things don't go to plan. They don't typically take constructive criticism well, and will deflect blame to others or to the circumstances of the situation. Dweck's research suggests people with this view, with fixed mindsets, significantly limit their potential for success.

However, if you have a growth mindset, you will typically believe that whatever level of intelligence or abilities you have, you can work on developing them through dedicated effort and hard work. People with growth mindsets have a love of learning, actively seek and accept constructive criticism well, place high importance on the effort they put into whatever they are doing, and tend to be more resilient when things don't go to plan. Dweck's research suggests that most, if not all, successful people have the qualities of a growth mindset.

The reality is, you can have both fixed and growth mindsets, depending on the context. For example, you might have a fixed mindset when it comes to playing sport. Your inner dialogue, or what you say to yourself might sound like, "I'm just not good at sport, I'm not athletic, I'm clumsy, and no matter how much I try, I won't get any better".

Whereas, although you might have a fixed mindset when it comes to sport, you could also have a growth mindset when it comes to business. Your inner dialogue might go something like, "No matter what the problem, I'm confident I can either find the solution or will be able to apply myself to learn something new that will help me solve the problem".

Long-term successful selling and the delivery of outstanding customer experiences starts firmly with your growth mindset.

What are you saying to yourself about your potential for success? What are you saying to yourself about how your skills, knowledge and attributes will help you be successful in your role? What are you saying about your capacity to learn and develop in your skills, knowledge and attributes? What are you saying about the value you create for your customers when you sell your products, service or advice to them?

Your belief in the value you can create for your customers when they buy what you sell, can have a direct and significant impact on how you 'feel' about selling what you sell. How you silently feel about selling what you sell can have a direct and significant impact on the activities you choose to implement, and on your ability and success in implementing them.

How to develop your growth mindset

Based on Dweck's research, here are four ways to develop a growth mindset:

Step 1: Tune into your self-talk. When you're facing a challenge in the activities you need to undertake to find, win or keep clients, ask yourself what you are silently saying to yourself about your capacity to do the task, or what others might think of you if you do the task. When things aren't going to plan, tune into how you're accepting (or not) any constructive criticism, or whether you're placing blame on others or on the circumstances of the situation.

What's your belief about the value you create when customers buy what you recommend?

Step 2: Accept that you have a choice. Whatever the situation, you really do have a choice about how you think about it. Will you choose to think with a fixed or with a growth mindset? Research by psychologist Dr Russ Harris[10] points out that a thought is just a thought and a feeling is just a feeling, and when you have negative thoughts and/or negative feelings you still have the choice to take positive action toward your goals.

An example of this can be seen in people who fear or at least have a little apprehension or get anxious about public speaking. They might think negative thoughts and get those feelings of nervousness, but they can still choose to stand in front of a group and deliver their presentation. Over time, with practice and coaching, I've known many people with a fear of public speaking who have been able to present effectively and professionally despite still feeling nervous. They simply manage and accept those thoughts and feelings and go on and do their presentation anyway.

Step 3: Apply a growth mindset alternative to whatever fixed mindset self-talk you're hearing. This is not merely constructing an affirmation to 'battle' against negative self-talk. You can make all the affirmations you want, but if you're making affirmations with a fixed mindset they're just positive words that you probably won't believe and, therefore, are less likely to take action on.

This step is about considering your level of competence, the resources you have at your disposal, and your willingness to apply your competence and resources to do what needs to be done. It's about considering what new skills or knowledge you might need to work on, or who you might need to ask for help.

Applying a growth mindset to a challenge is to avoid blame or playing the victim. It's a commitment to finding a way that can work for you.

Step 4: Take action based on your growth-mindset thinking. If you've seriously considered the first three steps, the only thing left to do, – which will take energy and effort, fuelled by your motivation to succeed – is to choose to take positive action. The question is, what actions and strategies will help you to achieve more new, repeat and referral sales?

As my Dad says, "If you want to get stuff done... do stuff!"

Four essential elements to a sales and customer service business

Let's dig a little deeper into how your fixed or growth mindset might impact your success as a salesperson or customer service provider.

When you think about it, successful selling shouldn't be that difficult. As you'll learn in this book, start with a clear and positive intention for your customers, create environments of opportunity to connect emotionally and intellectually with them, earn their trust by demonstrating your understanding of their wants and needs, provide solutions that will create value for them at a price they agree with, and help them to make comfortable and confident buying decisions that are in their best interest.

Simple? Yes. Easy? Not always!

In chapter one I suggested business success is determined by your capacity to find, win and keep customers. That's pretty much it ... find them, win them, keep them.

First, you've got to **find customers**, and there are basically two ways to do this.

One way is to proactively market, network, advertise, and promote your business, your products, services or advice. To do this you use a combination of online and traditional approaches to connect and engage with people who may want or need what it is you sell, or through referral partners and centres of influence who can provide access to people who may need or want what you sell.

The other way to find customers is in the development and delivery of an exceptional buying experience for them. This is about creating such a story, such a brand, through delivering on your promises of giving value, that your customers not only trust you, but are moved to want to refer others to you.

The second strategic element of business is to **win customers**. This is the major focus of this book. How do you communicate and engage with customers, with business and referral partners and centres of

Three essential activity goals for business success: find, win and keep customers.

influence, in ways that will help them to see the real value you can provide for them, and to create a buying experience where customers feel comfortable and confident to buy?

Applying the process of Building Customer Trust is directly aimed to help you succeed in winning customers.

The third strategic element of business is to **keep customers**. This is the core focus of delivering exceptional customer experiences both during and after the sale. Looping back into the first element of finding customers, this is the way we do what we do to earn loyalty, advocacy and more repeat and referral business.

When you think of any business, these three strategic elements – find, win and keep customers – are fundamentally what every business, profession and not-for-profit organisation needs to do.

There is, however, a fourth strategic element of business that will impact on your success. I refer to this as **managing self**. If you can't manage yourself, especially in disruptive and competitive business environments, quite simply the work of finding, winning and keeping customers just won't get done ... at least, not as successfully as it could.

The way you manage yourself in activities to find, win and keep clients will be directly and significantly impacted by the activity goals you set and pursue.

What we know from behavioural science research is that humans are aspirational, goal-seeking beings.[11] If you have set and are pursuing goals that are aligned with and support your personal sense of value and view of self, you are giving yourself a much better chance to flourish in your life than if you don't set and pursue personally aligned goals.

There is an important distinction that needs to be made here about goals.

Most sales and service people do not have control over their revenue or sales targets. This is also the experience of many sales and service managers. The sales targets are quite often set by an Executive Board. However, where leaders of sales and service teams can have a significant amount of control, is over the activities their teams undertake to achieve those mandatory sales and revenue targets.

Setting clear, measurable and accountable activity goals will significantly and positively impact your sales success and I recommend you adopt the well-proven activity of a daily 'To do' list.

Using our four strategic elements of business success (find, win, keep customers and managing self) you can set up a 'To do' list with these headings and hold yourself accountable each day (managing self) for achieving activity goals to find, win and keep customers.

Depending on your sales or service role, these activity goals might include the number of potential buyers and customers you aim to meet on a daily or weekly basis. It could be the number of phone calls, emails, proposals or quotes that you will aim to complete on a daily or weekly basis. It could be the number of networking events or association meetings you will attend and the number of new business cards you will collect to build your referral and collaborative networks. Or it could be the number of customers you aim to personally serve in a day.

As a researcher in applied positive psychology, I'm still astounded that despite the vast array of scientific evidence demonstrating the association between goal pursuit and human flourishing, there are still a significant number of people who report they do not have personal goals they are actively pursuing.

In this book I have referred to the importance of setting activity goals in a business context. However, what we know from the research is that setting and pursuing personal goals that help bring more meaning to your life will boost your wellbeing and this will have a positive impact on your broader mindset and motivation at work.

So, let me challenge you by asking to what extent you are setting and pursuing activity goals in your professional and personal life.

In this chapter so far I've highlighted the importance of having a growth mindset rather than a fixed mindset, and have touched on the value of setting and pursuing activity goals to find, win and keep clients.

We now turn to one of the most important elements essential for your sales and service success, and fundamental to you being able to apply the process of Building Customer Trust.

Professor Richard Ryan and Professor Edward Deci are the founders of a theory of motivation known as Self-Determination Theory[12], which provides an important guide to what it really takes to manage ourselves.

The importance of your self-determination

You're now more aware that people with growth mindsets tend to put in more effort and tend to be more resilient when things don't go the way they'd planned. Expanding on this for a moment, people with growth mindsets have an understanding and acceptance that while you can't control everything that happens in your life, you have the capacity to control how your respond and react to what happens. This is fundamentally what self-determination is all about.

While it is easy to say, "It's not what happens to you, but what you do about it that will make all the difference in your personal and professional success", it isn't in reality all that easy to live up to. Your sense of self-determination, however, is what will help you adopt and succeed with this important approach to life.

Deci's and Ryan's research highlights three essential ingredients that together form your sense of self-determination. They are your sense of *autonomy*, *competence* and *relatedness*. To get an understanding of Self-Determination Theory and the importance of your self-determination to your success, consider these three questions and score yourself on a rating scale of 1 being a low score and 10 being a high score:

In life, you can't always control what happens to you, but you do have the capacity to control how you respond and react to what happens.

Question 1: To what extent do you believe you have personal control over the activities you choose to do in your role as a leader, salesperson or customer service provider, and that these activities are aligned with your personal values and sense of self?

Question 2: To what extent do you believe you have the competence and resources at your disposal to successfully undertake the activities required of you in your role as a leader, salesperson or customer service provider?

Question 3: To what extent have you developed meaningful relationships that support you in successfully undertaking the activities required of you in your role as a leader, salesperson or customer service provider?

Question 1 refers to your sense of autonomy. Question 2 refers to your sense of competence. Question 3 refers to your sense of relatedness.

Deci's and Ryan's research suggests that these three elements of autonomy, competence and relatedness are innate needs that directly impact your motivation to get things done. When you think about this for a moment, it just makes sense. If you don't believe you've got any control over the activities you're undertaking to achieve your sales and revenue targets, or if what you're being asked to do is not aligned with what you think you ought to be doing, or not aligned with your personal values, you just won't be very motivated to give it your best.

Along the same line of thinking, if you don't believe you've got the competence or resources to complete the activities you need to achieve your sales or service delivery targets, it just makes sense that you won't be as motivated to give it your best, because you don't think you'll be able to do it anyway.

And finally, if you don't think that you've got supportive relationships that will help you complete the activities you need to complete to achieve your sales targets, your motivation will again be undermined.

If you've got issues with all three of these elements – autonomy, competence and relatedness – you're just going to struggle, and especially struggle in environments that are highly competitive and disruptive.

So how do you develop your sense of self-determination? This is where your intentions can help.

What we've learned from an at-work scientific experiment[13] within one of Australia's largest insurance companies is that there is an association between having and living up to positive intentions for your clients and enhanced levels of self-determination.

What you'll discover in the following chapters are a number of ways to gain clarity on your positive intentions for your customers (what you want *for* customers, not what you want from them) and ways to hold yourself accountable for delivering or living up to those intentions.

As you put these strategies in place, your sense of self-determination will increase, your capacity to better manage whatever life presents you with will become stronger, and your sense of meaning and purpose in the value you create when you sell what you sell will provide you with the momentum to win more new, repeat and referral sales.

So, let's start that journey of discovery and development now, as I introduce you to the Building Customer Trust blueprint.

CHAPTER SUMMARY

- Your mindset impacts your success
- You can choose a fixed or growth mindset
- Humans are aspirational, goal-seeking beings
- High levels of self-determination:
  - ignite motivation
  - increase proactive and reactive resilience
  - promote human flourishing
- Having positive intentions for customers builds your sense of self-determination

4

The Building Customer Trust process

YOUR SUCCESS AS A SALES OR SERVICE PERSON will depend on a combination of your intentions, beliefs, attitude, skills, knowledge and, as I highlighted in the previous chapter, a focus on finding, winning, keeping customers and managing yourself to do those three core activities better.

It's pretty much common sense. Unfortunately, over the years, much of the training and education of sales and service people has focused on manipulative communication techniques all geared to put pressure or coerce the customer into buying.

The problem with techniques is that they are just that: techniques!

When techniques are employed to get a sale instead of the sale being based on principles that the sales or service person is using to intentionally discover and meet their customers' needs, the techniques can establish barriers between the sales or service person and their customers.

When you think about it, no one likes to be *techniqued.*

Customers want to buy with confidence ...

They don't want to be 'techniqued'

No techniques or scripts

You will find the Building Customer Trust process has no scripts and is not based on techniques. It doesn't focus on how to close sales more quickly and more often, or how to get customers saying 'yes' all the time to prime them for the big yes at the close.

It's not relying on clever words or phrases or on using non-verbal influencing movements to increase the chance of a quick sale.

Having trained many thousands of sales and service people and leaders, what I know is that most sales and service people don't want to employ tricky sales techniques or manipulative closing strategies.

They want to be themselves, and project a positive image of themselves to their customers that states loud and clear,

"I'm the kind of person you can trust and will want to do business with!"

Using the Building Customer Trust process will help you plan for and review every opportunity to meet or be in contact with your customers. It will also help ensure you constantly deliver value for your customers and continually distance you from your competitors.

The BASICS of Building Customer Trust

Let me now introduce you to the Building Customer Trust process. Each letter in the acronym BASICS represents a step or principle in a customer-focused approach to sales, service, account management and communicating with people.

If you're an experienced sales or service professional, you'll be able to use the Building Customer Trust process as a review to help you reflect on and inspect your habits of success.

If you're relatively new to sales or service, you'll be able to use the process as a blueprint to boost your success.

The steps are:

Build trust	to create a trust-based customer experience
Ask questions	to identify customer needs and wants
Show value	by tailoring and presenting your recommendations
Identify obstacles	and work collaboratively to overcome them
Confirm next steps	to gain confirmation to proceed
Stay in touch	to ensure you've met customer expectations

In this chapter we'll start with Build trust and then you'll have the opportunity in the following chapters to explore each of the other steps in the Building Customer Trust process.

You will be introduced to the objectives of each step, as well as three action principles to implement the ideas and strategies designed to help you engage with your customers more confidently, comfortably, consistently and commercially.

As highlighted in previous chapters, most sales and service leaders and their teams get the importance of being able to build trust.

However, what you need to determine is how you will know when you've achieved a level of trust that will help the customer feel more comfortable and confident to make a wise buying decision?

The objective of this first step in the Building Customer Trust process is to create a comfortable, trust-based communication and customer experience.

The action principles to achieve this objective are:

1. Define and communicate your intention
2. Remove all distractions
3. Help set and manage customer expectations.

The first of our action principles is to *define and communicate your intention.*

The importance of defining and communicating your intention for your customers has been referred to previously. It's now time to delve more deeply into just why your intention for your customer is so important.

In the previous chapter I mentioned an at-work scientific experiment that linked a positive intention for customers with an increase in employee self-determination (their sense of autonomy, relatedness and competence). As a sales or service person, if you develop and hold yourself accountable for delivering on a positive intention for your customers your personal sense of self-determination – how you feel about who you are and what you represent to the world – will grow stronger.

Developing a positive intention for your customers is also a practical way to fast-track the trust-building process.

When you think about this deeply, you'll realise it just makes sense. If you have a genuine and positive intention to help customers achieve their goals, solve their problems, fulfil their wants or needs, and to make life better for them in some way, your customers will pick up on that intention.

I've mentioned several times that People Get Your Truth. This is the platform principle of what I refer to as Intentionomics ... the economics or value of your intentions.

Over time, your intentions, promises, actions and results will either promote you as trustworthy or expose you as being untrustworthy.

Trust building starts with your mindful awareness of what you intend to do, why you intend to do it, and a conscious awareness of the impact your intended actions will have on others.

In sales and service what this means is that by being mindfully aware of your intention for your customers – what you want for your customers, not what you want from them – you will have established the foundation for trust.

I recommend you take a moment right now to develop your own positive intention statement by thinking and making note of what you want for your customers. What do you want your customers to experience when they buy what you sell? What do you hope for your customers? What do you wish for them? Thinking about your answers to these questions, you'll be able to arrive at your own personal customer intention statement.

Here are a few examples from sales and service people I've coached in this process:

Financial adviser: *My intention for my clients is that they feel comfortable and confident their financial plan will help them achieve their lifestyle goals.*

Pharmaceutical product specialist: *My intention for my general practitioners is they are fully aware of how our product(s) can help their patients become and stay healthier.*

Retail sales or service professional: *My intention for my customers is that they enjoy their buying experience in our store, are thrilled with their purchase and what they buy meets or exceeds their expectations.*

When you read each of these you'll see that the focus is on what the sales or service person wants for their customers and not what they want from them.

Even if you don't personally like the above examples, remember, these sales or service people developed their intentions for their customers in their language and their context. Your intentions, language and context may be quite different.

Now it's your turn. Use the template below to write out your own personal intention statement for your customers.

Customer intention statement

My intention (my wish, hope, goal) for my customers is that they:

_____

_____

_____

_____

_____

Getting clear about your customer intention statement helps you to focus every communication opportunity you have with your customers on meeting and, wherever possible, exceeding their expectations. It will help you Build Customer Trust.

Imagine if you were meeting a financial adviser for the first time and she said to you, very early in the meeting, something like this: *I always like to let my clients know why I do what I do and what I genuinely want for them ... you see a financial plan is just a plan, but what I want for each and every one of my clients is they feel comfortable and confident that their financial plan that's created specifically for them, will help them achieve their lifestyle goals.*

I've coached and trained thousands of sales and service people from a vast range of industries and professions to write out their own customer intention statement and to weave it into their early discussions with new and existing customers.

This process helps build rapport and trust; it puts the customers at ease. In this financial adviser example, it helps the client understand the adviser's purpose or why they are a financial adviser, and to know that the financial adviser has the client's best interest as their driving motivation.

This process of starting with a clear and positive customer intention will help you to fast-track trust.

In the Building Customer Trust process the second action principle is to *remove all distractions*.

One of the challenges that often occurs for many sales or service people is to be mindfully present when communicating with customers.

To be mindfully present sounds easy, but many people struggle with it. Have you ever been in a conversation with someone, only to find as you're listening to them, your mind has wandered off and you've missed what they've just said? This is something most of us have experienced.

One practical way to practise active listening and to be mindfully present when you're in conversations with your customers is to develop a habit to help you listen.

It might be that when you've asked a question of a customer the practice of picking up your pen to write (or opening your note screen on your tablet) is your trigger or reminder to actively listen.

If taking notes isn't appropriate in your sales or service situation you might hold your hands in a certain way. My personal process is when I ask a question or someone is sharing something with me in my conference presentations, I place my right thumb in the palm of my left hand. This is my trigger to actively listen. I don't hold my right thumb in the palm of my left hand at any other time.

As you listen to what your customers have to say, it's also a powerful practice to listen for what they don't say. Listen to how they feel. Listen to the trivial things, which just might enable you to make a sale or retain a customer's ongoing business.

This action principle – to remove all distractions – is more than just common courtesy. It's about ensuring you personally are not distracted, as well as making sure there is nothing around you when you meet with the customer that could distract them from telling you exactly what it is they're after.

Active listening isn't always easy, but the more you practise it, the more sales you will make!

The third action principle in the Building Customer Trust process is to *help set and manage customer expectations*. You'll remember the first buyer exit ramp is the Initial Contact exit ramp, which is where the customer silently asks themselves the question, "What is this buying experience going to be like?"

First impressions – how to help set and manage buyer expectations

The power of first impressions is something that many of us know, but sometimes forget. The saying goes, you only get one chance to make a favourable first impression, but you have chances every day to build on the impressions you make with your clients.

Here are 10 points on managing first impressions to consider. I don't go into each of these points in detail. They've been provided for you to think about some of the more practical elements that contribute to building trust. Take a moment to reflect on your own buying experiences, your selling and customer engagement approach, and how you currently engage with a customer early in the conversation to build trust.

1. The handshake: This is more related to business-to-business and professional advising, as it is less likely for retail sales and customer service people to shake hands with their clients ... although that may not always be the case. People interpret many things from your handshake. For example, what if you've got what you believe to be a professional handshake but the person receiving it interprets it as a "bone crusher" (too strong or forceful)? What if you've got what you believe to be a professional handshake but the person receiving it interprets it as a "limp and soft" handshake?

The point here is that we tend to shake hands the way *we* like to shake hands. That's why we get to interpret all those 'funny' handshakes we receive. Think about this for a moment; it can be very enlightening. Let's assume that most people want to give a favourable first impression. Often, one of the ways this is conveyed is through a handshake. Why then do we find so many different handshakes

What's the first impression you're hoping to create when you first meet with customers?

when we meet people? The answer is that most people are shaking hands the way they personally like to shake hands ... and the other person might like to shake hands differently.

Without belabouring the point, if the person you're about to meet has a strong handshake, be ready for it. If the person you're about to meet has a soft handshake, be ready for it also. This is what one of my mentors, Ron Willingham, refers to as 'Starting in neutral'.

Now, this is less about the handshake itself or a commentary on body language, and more about a useful metaphor around building trust. The metaphor is simply that by starting in neutral, you're trying to communicate with the customer in ways they like. If they want detail, be happy to provide them with detail. If they want big picture, be happy to provide them with big picture.

When you start in neutral and with a clear intention to make life better for your customer in some way, you're ready to build trust by truly being customer focused.

2. Environment: Again, this is more relevant for business-to-business or professional advisers who have the privilege of meeting in the client's home or office. Notice and use, when appropriate, what you observe about their personal environment. Be careful here, though. Don't invade people's emotional space by prying, or assuming you can start talking about personal things you notice in their environment.

Generally, when the client raises personal or lifestyle information, it may be an indication they would like to chat about the topic – but tread carefully. Many sales and service people try to become too friendly too quickly; this results from using the principle of building trust as a technique and not as a genuine attempt to be customer focused.

3. Eye contact: When you're face to face with a customer, your eye contact is important. In most western cultures it is customary to pay people the respect of looking them in the eye when you talk with them. That can be difficult if you're taking notes and recording important information that the customer is telling you, but in general you want to maintain good eye contact.

4. What you wear: Does the image you project match with what your customers expect? Are you making definite statements about your personal brand? This may seem a trivial point, but it's amazing once you look around you, just how often you see little things about a sales or service person's appearance that can cause customers to be distracted. For example, bracelets that continually bang on a desk in an interview, or frayed collars on shirts, or ties that belong in another era, or unpolished or worn-out shoes.

5. Talk to the person: Are you focused and demonstrating that you are genuinely interested in your customer? Remember to keep coming back to the specific situation for this person. Don't talk too generally. Don't talk too much about others. Always come back to what is important and specific to the individual customer's situation.

6. Open and friendly: Yes, this is business; but let them get a sense of the real you. Again, this may seem a bit simple, but a genuine smile goes a long way in building strong emotional and intellectual connections with people. Not cheesy, false grins put on because you think it's necessary, but genuine, happy facial expressions that demonstrate your belief in who you are, what you sell and the value you can create – why wouldn't you want to be smiling?

7. Not over the top: As mentioned earlier with the handshake, start communicating in neutral and then turn to ways that help make the customer comfortable. Just be careful not to be too energetic, laid back or reserved. Get a feel for how the customer likes to communicate and, without trying to mirror their every move (they'll ask if you've been to a body language workshop!), just be aware of the impact of your own body language on the way the two of you are communicating.

8. Starting the conversation: If you're a natural conversationalist, starting conversations won't be a problem for you. But if you're not, trying to fake it is a flawed approach. In business-to-business or professional advice situations, start the conversation with your intention and outline what you are hoping to cover or achieve, and then ask the customer what they're hoping to cover or achieve? While

Building trust doesn't mean you need to master the art of 'small talk'. Many customers will be comfortable in just getting down to business.

asking "How may I help you?" certainly isn't the worst way to start a conversation, in certain sales or service situations the customer won't really know how you can be of help to them. What they're after is someone who can help them discover what they want or need.

9. Belief in the value you create: If you don't believe in the value you create, how will your customers? This is a larger topic than just a couple of lines in this chapter. Remember that earlier we explored how your thoughts can affect your feelings, which can affect your actions, your habits and your success. What do you believe about the value you create when you sell what you sell?

10. Body language: Be aware of what messages you send with your non-verbals, but don't get sucked into reading the body language of others as if every movement they make means something. Some people just like to sit with their arms crossed – they're comfortable (or cold!). It doesn't mean they are necessarily closed to what you're saying. If they sit forward in their chair, it doesn't mean that they're necessarily interested in the point you're making – it could mean that they just needed to shift from one cheek to the other to get more comfortable on the seat ... hopefully you're getting the picture. With all due respect to the body language gurus, it's all a bit too much pop psychology. Having said that, if you find your customers standing and leaving while you're in conversation with them ... I'd probably interpret that as a no!

Building trust isn't coming up with the one best opening line. It isn't about finding the one or two best opening questions. It's about the intention, attitude and purpose behind why you're calling, meeting or communicating with the customer. When you meet with someone, your prime purpose should be to gain (or reconfirm) their trust. Building a long-term business relationship starts with earning trust, and then building on that trust over time.

This first step of the Building Customer Trust process is the foundation for all other steps. You won't be able to get great information from your customers if they first haven't felt like they have some level of rapport and trust with you.

When you go out in the field, meet in your office or communicate with customers in your store, this chapter is asking you to consider how well you build trust and rapport. It's at this first step in the Building Customer Trust process that your intention, morals, values and attitude become evident to your customers.

People Get Your Truth. Over time, your intentions, promises, actions and results will either promote you as trustworthy or expose you as not.

On the following page, and at the end of each of the following chapters, you have an opportunity to complete a self-assessment.

This has been designed to help you identify your areas of strength and areas of potential improvement. I recommend that you complete the self-assessment as you read each chapter, and discuss your ratings with your colleagues or manager.

Circle a number from 1 – 5 to indicate your personal rating for each statement. Rating Key: 1 = Never, 2 = Rarely, 3 = Occasionally, 4 = Often, 5 = Always

Build trust:

I am able to 'break the ice' easily with customers	1	2	3	4	5
I can help customers quickly become comfortable with me	1	2	3	4	5
I ensure I don't invade a customer's physical or emotional space	1	2	3	4	5
I am able to 'connect' emotionally and intellectually with customers	1	2	3	4	5
I am aware how my personal style impacts others	1	2	3	4	5
I am able to sum up a customer's style quickly and accurately	1	2	3	4	5
I am able to gain customer trust rather quickly when I first meet with them	1	2	3	4	5
I usually spend more time listening than talking when I first meet with customers	1	2	3	4	5
I have standard questions to ask during the opening phase when I meet with customers	1	2	3	4	5
I am aware of the impact of my non-verbal communication when I meet with customers	1	2	3	4	5

Interpretation and Action Planning

The higher your score, the more likely this area is one of your strengths. To start a personal development action plan, look to the area(s) where you have rated yourself higher and set a goal(s) to build on that strength. Where you have rated yourself lower, set a goal(s) to improve in some way.

CHAPTER SUMMARY

‣   Develop a positive intention for customers
‣   Build your confidence for self-trust, your courage to trust in others and your combined character and competence to earn the trust of others.
‣   The first step in the Building Customer Trust process is to Build trust
‣   People Get Your Truth! Over time, your intentions, promises, actions and results will either promote you as trustworthy or expose you as untrustworthy

5

The power of value-discovery questions

THE SECOND STEP in the Building Customer Trust process is to Ask questions.

The objective of this step is to help both customer and sales or service person clearly identify and clarify customer wants and needs.

The questions you ask your customers will demonstrate your intention as a sales or service professional. That's why getting clear on your intention (what you want *for* your customers, not what you want from them) is the foundation upon which the Building Customer Trust process rests.

As you consider the objectives of the Ask questions step, let's also consider how you would go about achieving these through the application of some action principles.

The action principles when implementing the objectives of this step are:

1. Ask appropriate information and value-discovery questions
2. Listen actively
3. Help clarify and prioritise wants and needs.

Let's consider each of these action principles, starting with asking appropriate information and value-discovery questions.

It's obvious to most leaders and their sales or service teams that it's important to ask questions to find out what the customer is after (although, as consumers most of us realise it's more obvious to some sales or service people than it is to others).

However, this begs the question: What type of questions do we need to ask?

You might have heard the saying, 'There's no such thing as a dumb question'. Well, I don't agree with that. Maybe in learning environments there's no such thing as a dumb question, but in the business world, and certainly in the world of sales and service, there are dumb questions that we should avoid asking at all costs.

Questions to avoid

OK, maybe dumb question is a bit harsh. But at the very least there are unskilled questions to avoid.

Your purpose in asking questions is to create value for your customers, to build further rapport and trust, and to deepen the level of understanding between the customer and yourself.

You therefore want to ensure you ask appropriate questions that do not disengage the customer from the conversation.

How do you know whether you're about to ask a question that could potentially disengage a customer from the conversation? One way is to ensure your questions do not have the potential of the client responding (either out loud or to themselves), "Of course!"

Here's an example:

When we were renovating our home, Liz and I went to a major retail store that sold household appliances. We were in the refrigerator section of the store – there was nothing else around us, just fridges.

In business, there are such things as 'dumb questions', or at the very least, unskilled questions that add no value to building customer trust.

We'd been there for about ten minutes when finally a salesperson came up to us and asked, "Are you interested in a fridge?"

My internal reaction was, "Of course – what else am I here for – the lawnmowers?" But I refrained from saying it out loud.

My point is, why else would we be in the fridge section? The sales assistant's question did not help or add value to our conversation – it had fractured the flow of conversation and rapport.

Here's another example. Liz and I had two financial advisers from a mortgage broking firm come to our home to discuss getting a mortgage loan to fund a property we were considering buying.

They turned up on time, but they both looked like they'd been sleeping in their shirts from the creases they had, and one of them had that little piece of plastic sticking out of a frayed collar. The other one had not even bothered to shave that day. Quite frankly, on first impression I had already decided not to do business with them. However, Liz is a lot nicer than me, so we invited them in to see if they could help us.

About five minutes into their presentation, finally one of them looked at Liz and asked the first question in our conversation. He asked, "Liz, is dealing with someone you can trust important to you?"

My inner thoughts shouted, "Of course," but Liz was quicker than I was; she looked directly back at him and said, "No ...we're looking for someone who is untrustworthy – can you help us?"

What a ridiculous question. Of course dealing with someone we could trust would be important to us. Anyway, we soon ended the conversation and didn't do any business with that firm.

My point is this: The questions you ask are direct windows to your intention for your customers. Your questions demonstrate to your customers what your true purpose is. Are you there simply to talk about your products or services in the hope of a sale? Or are you there to learn about your customer's specific needs and discover whether you can help them in any way?

On another occasion (maybe I just attract these types of salespeople?) we sought out a cement renderer for a property we were renovating. He didn't get the job because he asked me, "Is a quality finish important to you, David?" Of course a quality finish is important to me. I'm sure very few people would ever answer otherwise, unless they were a dodgy property developer looking to flip a house without caring about the people buying it.

Later in this chapter we will look at how to construct powerful value-discovery questions. For now, however, we'll consider the remaining action principles in the Ask questions step of the Building Customer Trust process.

Listen actively ... really listen!

The second action principle for the Ask questions step is to listen actively.

Building on our discussion in the previous chapter on listening, some people are natural listeners; others have mind traffic that clogs their capacity to listen.

Whenever you ask a question of a customer, your capacity to really listen is going to have a significant impact on your overall success. If you're in business-to-business sales or professional advising, asking permission to take some notes as your clients begin to answer questions is a great way to actively listen to what they are saying.

Even when taking physical notes isn't appropriate – for example that would just look a bit weird in a retail store environment – taking mental notes is still important.

As you ask questions of your customers and really listen to their answers, you can help them clarify and prioritise their needs, so you can present more tailored solutions for them to achieve their goals.

This is the third of our action principles in the Ask questions step of the Building Customer Trust process.

Help customers prioritise what's most important to them, so you can tailor every presentation and avoid talking about product or service features and benefits that aren't of value.

You demonstrate your capacity to help customers clarify and prioritise their needs by referring to your notes, or to your mental notes, of their answers to your questions, and say something like, "Well, these four things seem to be the key elements you're looking for. Which of these would you say is the most important to you?"

This gives you a framework for presenting your tailored solutions to their highest priority needs first, and then addressing each need in turn.

Let's now look at how you can go about crafting and then asking appropriate questions that have the capacity to create value for your customers.

Here's a quick exercise to get you thinking about the questions you are asking currently. Take a moment here to think back over the past week or so, as you've been meeting with existing and potential customers.

Make a list of three major questions you ask that really help you to build trust and understand the customers' needs or wants or specific situation. I encourage you not to just read this page. Take a moment and actually complete this exercise. You will gain value by doing this.

Once you've made a list of the questions, take a look at each of them and, on the same page, make a note of your purpose in asking each question. In other words, write down why you asked that question and what you were trying to learn, discover or achieve.

While you reflect on your questions and the purpose for each, ask yourself the following: *Would your client expect you to know the answer to any of the questions you asked?*

If the answer is yes, you may want to consider changing or not asking that question, because unless you're trying to confirm your understanding about something you ought to know already (and that would be a valid reason), asking a question the customer would expect you to know the answer to could be potentially a bit patronising.

Questions that have the potential to be patronising to a customer create apprehension and stress fractures in the emotional and intellectual connections that you are trying to build.

Do any of the questions you've asked have relatively obvious answers? If so, you may want to consider changing or not asking that question, because if you're asking questions that have relatively obvious answers, it creates the 'of course syndrome' in the customer's mind. Again, this can result in the customer feeling patronised.

If the answer to a question will obviously be, "Yes, of course", why would you want to ask that question? The result can be emotional or intellectual disconnect between you and your customer.

Your intention and purpose is quite clear once you start asking questions. For this reason you need to be comfortable, confident and proud of the questions you ask.

Many sales and customer engagement training courses in the past have focused on asking questions that will lead your customer to say "Yes" many times in a short period, or steer them to a predetermined path.

These types of questions may appear to be clever on the surface, and may even work in some situations – to a certain extent. However, there is a stronger chance that they will set you up for failure!

So, what should be the focus of your questions?

Plain and simple: Your focus should be to understand what's important to the customer, what their wants and needs are, what problems they have, or what goals they're trying to achieve.

You should not be looking for a predetermined answer. You should not expect one. The key principle here is to ask appropriate questions that add value and clarity to the conversation for both you and your customer.

In fact, if you ask powerful questions that have the capacity to *comfortably disturb* customers to take appropriate action to create personal value, you will achieve value early in your conversation.

Your intention and purpose become clear to customers once you start asking them questions.

In other words, your customers become so engaged in answering the questions you ask, they are gaining value from the conversation ... and you haven't even started to discuss products, services or solutions.

If the customer would expect you to know the answer to a question you're asking, or if it's an obvious answer, or if it seems to be pushing them toward a specific answer, then this question will just build a defensive wall between you and the customer.

The customer will see the questions for what they are – a technique that is not in their best interest – and this builds cynicism and mistrust between the customer and sales or service person.

The following exercise will help you design questions to help both you and your customers understand whether you can make a difference, add value, solve a problem or offer a solution for them.

Once again, I encourage you to complete this exercise and not simply read through it.

The process of developing value-discovery questions starts with you thinking about what benefits your customers receive, what value you create for them, and also what opportunities you create (or if you prefer, what problems you solve) for them if they buy what you sell or agree to proceed with your recommendations and advice.

So now, take a few moments and make notes on what customers really get from you. What is the real value, solution, need or want that is fulfilled when they buy what you sell or agree to proceed with your recommendations and advice?

Your answers should not be the names of the products or services you provide. They should be what your customers receive when they buy those products or services or accept and take action on your advice.

Have you made a list? If so, well done!

Look at what you've recorded. What you have just created is a series of *value units*, or value propositions, that you offer customers.

The more clarity you have in the value you can create through the value units or value propositions, the more readily you will be able to articulate these to your customers in ways that will engage them, and encourage them to take appropriate action to receive the value they seek from you.

Here's a list of 52 value units of what our research suggests customers are looking for when they buy important products or services. Some of these will be appropriate for you, others may not be. However, the list ought to be of assistance in understanding the significant range of values you offer and that your customers receive, beyond the features of your products or service. We discuss this in more detail in the next chapter.

1. Education
2. Direction
3. Recognition
4. Reinforcement
5. Peace of mind
6. Reassurance
7. Hope
8. Clarity
9. Challenge
10. Opportunity
11. Check up
12. Reality check
13. Problem solving
14. Partnership
15. Goal management
16. Lifestyle choices
17. Sense of community
18. Process
19. Friend
20. Trust
21. Support
22. Information
23. Choice
24. Expertise
25. Guidance
26. Coach
27. Unreasonable friend
28. Financial security
29. Proof
30. Flexibility
31. History
32. Future
33. Experience
34. Personal contact (you)
35. Research
36. Management
37. Confidant
38. Recommendations
39. Confidence
40. Security
41. Belief
42. Personal success
43. Vision
44. Brand
45. Your network
46. Sounding board
47. Access
48. Ideas
49. Freedom
50. Structure
51. Validation
52. A plan for success

Whether you choose some of the value units listed above, or have arrived at some of your own, once you have a list of the real values, needs, wants and solutions you provide, you can design some questions that get your customers telling you whether or not these are important to them.

The key point of this exercise is that although all the responses you have recorded are what customers can receive from you, not all customers will find value in or want all that you've listed.

We want to discover, through asking questions, which of these needs, wants, value or solutions might be important for the customer you're with ... not for all customers.

Let's consider two examples – a destructive question and a constructive question:

One response you may have recorded is that when a customer buys what you sell, they receive quality.

OK then, let's test this out in a question.

A destructive question: "How important is quality to you?" Or even worse ... "Is quality important to you?"

These are redundant questions. Of course quality is going to be important to customers. Surely we live in an age when everyone just expects quality. This question will do your cause no favours at all. Your customers will be thinking, "What a ridiculous question to ask me!"

A constructive question: "When you have purchased (types of products or service you sell), how do you assess the overall quality you receive – what's most important to you?" Or "What is it you hope to experience when you (buy this product ... act on this advice ... implement this program ... receive this service)?"

Hopefully you can see the difference in these two approaches.

Not every feature or benefit will be of value to every customer. Your questions help you and your customers prioritise what's really of value.

Constructive questions are intentionally positive, they focus the customer's thoughts and feelings on problems they're wanting to solve, goals they're wanting to achieve, and will provide you with valuable information. Destructive questions simply don't create any valuable information and will more than likely just antagonise the customer and cause them to disconnect and take one of the buyer exit ramps we discussed earlier.

Now it's your turn.

Go back to each of the needs, wants, values or solutions you recorded earlier and start to develop some questions that get your customers thinking about the wants, needs, values and solutions they seek.

The question should be open ended; i.e. beginning with who, what, when, where, why, how, etc.

Remember, open-ended questions allow customers to open up and talk. Closed questions (usually allowing only a yes/no answer) restrict the conversation.

You will know when you have asked an effective question by the depth of the response from the customer. If you get too brief an answer, try probing with another open-ended question.

Here's an example of a question that has the capacity to comfortably disturb a customer. It is a mind-shifting type of question. It's a value-discovery question.

I first stumbled over this question after watching a video program titled *The Business of Paradigms*, by Joel Barker.[14] It's not so much that this is a question you need to be asking – in fact it may not be appropriate for your situation of selling at all – but there is a great lesson in understanding why the question is so powerful.

Here's the question: *What today is impossible for you to do in your business, that if it could be done, would change what you do for the better?*

I know ... it's a big question; but let me break it down into its component parts so you can understand why it is so powerful.

The first key component of the question is that it has a time perspective: "What today". It could have been, "What in the past twelve months" or "What in the next three weeks".

Helping customers clarify and confirm their current situation by reflecting on the past and looking into the future helps both you and the customer better understand what might be done to improve that situation, and how you might be able to help.

One of my clients from an engineering company discovered that changing this aspect of their question was very positive. They used to ask, "What are some problems you've experienced in the past with this type of equipment?" Their customers often brought up issues from so far in the past that they were no longer relevant – although they still bothered the customer. When they changed the question to, "Over the past twelve months, what are some problems you've experienced?" the customers were focused only on more relevant and recent issues.

The second key component of the question is focusing the customer on either a problem or opportunity. In this example it's "impossible for you to do". However, it could have been "difficult for you to achieve" or "you are aiming to achieve".

The point is, unless there is some form of current discomfort, something lacking, something not quite right for the customer, or something the customer is trying to achieve in the present or future, it's going to be difficult to sell them anything they will see of value.

You can't sell value unless you can first establish that there is a current lack of value or a desire to create future value in the customer's situation, and that they would like to receive that value.

This brings us to the third key component of the question, which is "in your business". This provides the customer with context.

The more specific the context within your question, the easier it is for your customer to answer. For example, instead of "in your business" it could be "in your personal life" or "in terms of managing your finances" or "using your time more effectively".

Your questions can help your customers focus on the future value they want to receive or experience.

The fourth key component of the question is "that if it could be done". This simply opens up the possibility and challenges the customer to think, "What if?"

In the question, we're not committing to doing anything about their situation just yet; we're helping to clarify whether, if the possibility were there, would it be something they would like to explore?

The fifth and final key component of the question is "for the better".

This focuses the customer on some sort of improved state. It's either fixing what is wrong or achieving what is being aimed at. It opens up the customer to explore and discuss ways to make their life better. If you can establish that their current situation isn't ideal, and that they are prepared to make some kind of positive change to achieve the result and value they seek, then you increase the value of the propositions you can offer.

Now, again, this is not so much about you learning or even liking this question. It's about the key components within this type of question.

Think deeply about the questions you ask.

Take time to structure your questions to have as many of these key components as possible and you'll be building deeper levels of rapport, trust and understanding between you and your customers.

Avoiding an interrogation

One of the biggest mistakes many sales or service people make is to ask too many questions.

Be careful not to bombard your customers with so many questions they feel like they're being interrogated. To avoid this, one of the recommended approaches in the Building Customer Trust process is, where appropriate, to share your experience and knowledge about key features, benefits and value that your customers are typically seeking and to ask them which of those are most important to them.

The conversation would go something like, "Based on my experience with other customers, there are typically these three (or five) things they're trying to achieve. Of those, which is most important to you?"

Of course, you'll need to reword that to fit your own sales or service context, but this is a powerfully effective way to demonstrate your knowledge of your customers' situations, expectations, wants and needs, and also demonstrate that you're wanting to help this customer to prioritise with you what's most important in their world.

Some key principles of asking questions

Some of the key principles that follow may be more applicable to you than others, depending on the business you are in. Look for ways you either have applied or could apply the principles.

For each statement, reflect on your last two or three meetings with your customers and answer the questions that follow each statement.

• *No one buys anything unless it fills a want or a need, solves a problem, helps them achieve an opportunity or goal, or represents value they seek.*

In your last two or three meetings, what have been the admitted needs, wants, problems or opportunities that your customers have expressed?

• *Open-ended questions help both you and your customers learn more about potential needs, wants, value or problems that your products and services might help them with.*

Reflect on the last two or three meetings you have had. For what percentage of these are you confident your customers articulated to you that they had a need or a want that they believed you could help them with?

• *Where appropriate, ask permission to take notes, and record what your customers say in response to your questions. This allows you to summarise, clarify and prioritise their wants and needs before moving on to the next step of showing the value you can offer.*

Over the past two or three meetings you have had with your customers, how well have you been able to prioritise their needs? What was most important to them? How do you know this?

• *It's important to notice customer reactions to your questions as well as their answers. Listen to the tone of their responses and gauge how they're feeling. Be careful not to get too caught up in trying to read their body language – focus on your questions, your positive customer intention, your sincerity, integrity and purpose in asking them.*

Over the past two or three meetings with your customers, what reactions did you notice, and how did you interpret their reactions?

So how are you at asking questions?

This chapter has recommended you ask appropriate questions. Really think about the quality of your questions and the degree to which they add value to the conversation and create clarity for both you and your customers.

As you reflect on your learning from this chapter, ideally you will have discovered or rediscovered ways to:

Spend time planning your questions. Try to arrive at two or three questions that will help both you and your customer better understand their needs and wants, and what you can do to help them.

Ask open-ended questions that help both you and your customer better understand their needs and wants, and what you can do to help them.

Listen actively and, where appropriate, ask permission to take notes during your conversations. Take down important points and use them to summarise your understanding of your customer's needs.

Work with your customer to **prioritise their needs**. You may identify a number of important points. Which of these would your customer like to focus on?

Finally, as you reflect on your past conversations with customers, and implement the suggestions above, keep the following tip in mind:

Highly successful sales or service people have learned that most of the trust building takes place while they're asking questions and listening to the answers of their customers. This means that the customer realises you are a person they want to do business with. They recognise that you're not there for your own reasons, but it truly is a win-win approach you are seeking.

The more you focus on trying to discover the needs and wants you may be able to help each customer achieve, the more they will realise this and they will drop their defensiveness, open up and communicate with you in the hope that you will be able to make a difference for them.

A quote I understand was originally said by Elvis Presley is, "Our values are like fingerprints. We all have them, but everyone's are different. And we leave them over everything we touch."

Said another way, and I realise I've repeated this a number of times, People Get Your Truth. Over time your intentions, promises, actions and results will either promote you as trustworthy, or expose you as untrustworthy.

It is through your questions that customers get to know your real intentions and values.

On the following page you have an opportunity to complete a self-assessment on the Ask questions step in the Building Customer Trust process.

Circle a number from 1 – 5 to indicate your personal rating for each statement. Rating Key: 1 = Never, 2 = Rarely, 3 = Occasionally, 4 = Often, 5 = Always					
Ask questions:					
I am always clear on my objectives for each customer meeting	1	2	3	4	5
I have developed several standard questions to ask during my customer meetings	1	2	3	4	5
I am confident and competent in discovering the true needs of my customers	1	2	3	4	5
I have a process that ensures I have understood my existing and potential customers' needs	1	2	3	4	5
The questions I ask are focused on discovering needs	1	2	3	4	5
My questions challenge customers to think beyond their immediate wants and needs	1	2	3	4	5
I am skilled at helping potential and existing customers prioritise their needs	1	2	3	4	5
The questions I ask reflect who I am and what I stand for	1	2	3	4	5
The questions I ask help to clarify what my business can offer a customer	1	2	3	4	5
The questions I ask help customers to distance me from my competitors	1	2	3	4	5

Interpretation and Action Planning

The higher your score, the more likely this area is one of your strengths. To start a personal development action plan, look to the area(s) where you have rated yourself higher and set a goal(s) to build on that strength. Where you have rated yourself lower, set a goal(s) to improve in some way.

CHAPTER SUMMARY

› Trust is built on the questions you ask
› Your value-discovery questions demonstrate to customers your intention for them
› Develop your questions with time perspective, possibility, context, and desired value
› Demonstrate your expertise by using a checklist approach to help customers prioritize their wants and needs

6

What it really means to show value

IN EACH OF THE STEPS in the Building Customer Trust process, you are behaviourally evidencing your positive intention for your customers. This is what enables you to fast-track trust.

If you've completed the Ask questions step effectively, and really listened to discover what your customers want and need, in the Show value step you'll be able to practically show your customers your intention is to make life better for them in some way.

Every presentation or recommendation you make to a customer will be tailored in ways to evidence your understanding of their wants and needs and your intention to deliver, meet and, where possible, exceed their expectations.

However, this is not what customers typically experience.

One of the more common complaints customers make about sales or service people is that they have a 'canned' or generic approach when talking about their products or services.

In other words, regardless of the context, wants or needs of the individual customer, the sales or service person pretty much says the same thing, almost like a well-rehearsed script to explain the features, benefits and assumed value of their products and services.

This is where the Building Customer Trust process really helps sales and service people as well as their customers to have a more meaningful and effective conversation.

Having completed the Build trust and Ask questions steps in the process, and understanding that you've prioritised what's most important to the customer, you're now able to discuss your products or services – the features and benefits – in ways that are tailored specifically for each customer you meet with.

If you haven't asked great questions and discovered specific needs, wants, opportunities or problems your customers want to solve, then what could you possibly talk about when presenting a product, service or solution to them?

Major check point!

To know you and your customer are ready to present your products and services in the Show value step, here are three key statements you will need to make to yourself:

Statement 1: "I now know what this customer is looking for."

Statement 2: "I understand what product or service will meet their needs."

Statement 3: "I now know which features of the product or service are most important to this customer and will deliver the end-result benefits that will be of value to them."

If you can't affirm these three statements to yourself, you're not ready for the Show value step; you're still in the Ask questions part of the process.

Objective of this step

The objective of the Show value step in the Building Customer Trust process is to tailor and present specific value and recommendations for each customer.

Once again, there are three action principles to help you implement and achieve this objective:

1. Discuss features and benefits to show tailored value
2. Be clear on what you can and can't promise
3. Seek feedback and opinions.

Before you start talking specifically about your products and services, don't waste the opportunity to demonstrate your understanding of what the customer is seeking.

If you've taken notes during your Ask questions step (or if more appropriate, you've been taking 'mental notes') you will be able to reconfirm the customer's prioritised needs and let them know how your product or service's features and benefits will achieve the value they are seeking.

Most importantly, the first action practice principle suggests you tailor solutions to the customer's specific situation.

Beyond a rehearsed and generic product or service presentation

Showing value isn't just demonstrating your products and services – or telling your customers how good your products and services are. Showing value is about tailoring every presentation or discussion to the customer's specific needs, wants and expectations.

To help you do this, let's spend a moment on one of the most important concepts that highly effective sales and service people understand: customers buy for their reasons ... not yours!

You already realise that people are different; they have different backgrounds, different experiences, different personalities and different lifestyle and business contexts. They also quite often will have different approaches to the way they buy things.

You can have two people who want the same product or service, but they will buy it for different reasons. If you miss the dominant reasons upon which each customer is making their buying decisions, you may miss the sale.

What drives people to make buying decisions?

Researchers Lawrence and Nohria[15] have completed a major review on what motivates or drives people to make decisions. Much of their research is summarised in their book, *Driven*.

Basically, they outline that people have four innate drives: to acquire things, to belong to groups, to understand or comprehend things in their life and to defend what is important to them.

This is a powerful framework for sales and service people to understand.

As you're asking your customers questions, listen for which of these drives seem to be more dominant than others. Do their answers reflect more about the importance of acquiring a specific brand, product or experience?

Do their answers reflect more about belonging or being associated with being 'on trend' or 'keeping up with the Joneses'?

Do their answers reflect more about wanting to understand or comprehend their professional or personal life?

Or do their answers reflect more about wanting to defend their current lifestyle or business goals?

In addition to the research by Nohria and Lawrence, there is a host of other scientific research around personality styles, communication styles and buying styles. Here is a summary of four styles of

Customers buy for their
reasons, not yours!

communicating that people typically choose, depending on their context.

Notice I'm saying "choose". This is important for anyone in sales and service to understand. People choose how they buy. It is not necessarily their natural communication or personality style. When customers are buying something that is important to them, they may adopt a 'buyer style' of communicating.

The good news is that the Building Customer Trust process guides you in being able to Show value to your customers in a way that will be aligned with their preferred buying style.

The four 'styles' of buyer that I will highlight here are Social, Active, Steady and Reserved. In reality, your customers (and you) are likely to be a combination of these four styles.

Social: These people tend to be outgoing, chatty, openly friendly and warm. They love being involved with other people and social events. They seek friendship, love to do lunch or meet over coffee or tea, and place high emphasis on talking things through (they love to talk). They may appear to be unorganised; they do not like conflict situations and tend to be openly emotional about things.

Who do you know – maybe a customer or colleague – who on the surface seems to be a Social style of person?

Active: These people are driven by success and the appearance of being successful. They are extremely active, quick paced and ready to move onto the next important job (sometimes forgetting about finishing the last one). They are strongly tuned into station WIIFM (What's In It For Me) and are results driven. They do not like too much detail. They will visually or verbally remind others of their success (occasional yet well-placed namedropping, snappy clothing, expensive-looking jewellery, trophies, awards, etc.).

Who do you know who on the surface seems to be an Active style of person?

Steady: These people do not like to be pushed or rushed. They enjoy systems and processes. Attention to detail and procedural adherence is their catch cry. They usually do not like to take risks, and will take their time to assess all possible outcomes of a situation before deciding. They enjoy reading brochures, specifications and detail and understanding how things work, and the process that will be in place.

Who do you know who on the surface seems to be a Steady style of person?

Reserved: These people are bottom-line and facts based. They tend to keep their ideas and feelings to themselves, and can be turned off by highly energetic and emotional people. They value time and reflection. They often want to have proof about a course of action or suggestion; they enjoy playing devil's advocate and tend to ask lots of 'why' questions.

Who do you know who on the surface seems to be a Reserved style of person?

Dominant deciding values

Let's consider each of these four styles – social, active, steady and reserved – and explore how they are associated with a person's dominant deciding values – values that help them decide what they will buy, why they will buy it, and from whom they will buy it.

To make it easier for you to remember these, I've labelled these dominant deciding values as the Five Es of Buying.

Most, if not all, customers want and expect a good price and value. That is, they have a deciding value based on *economics*. However, depending on their style and context, there are four other deciding values that usually need to be satisfied before a client even gets to worrying about price.

Each customer chooses the way they want to communicate and buy from you. Make sure you're selling the way they want to buy!

Social style people have a dominant deciding value of *enjoyment*. They can get products and services from lots of different people, but generally their strongest deciding value of enjoyment is the first bridge any sales or service person will need to build.

In other words, Social style people will want to like you and feel a strong rapport with you, before they worry about price or other points of difference.

Active style people have a dominant deciding value of *ego*. They also can get their products and services from lots of different people, but generally their strongest deciding value of ego is the first bridge any sales or service person will need to build.

Active style people will want to have a strong sense of 'image connection' with you, your work environment and your approach. They will want you to recognise their own importance and special image before they worry about price, enjoyment or other points of difference.

Steady style people have a dominant deciding value of *ease*. Generally their strongest deciding value of ease is the first bridge any sales or service person will need to build.

Steady style people will want to feel at ease with you, safe with what you're saying and secure about the purchase (warranty, guarantee, follow-up service). This will be a higher priority for them than price, enjoyment or ego.

Reserved style people have a dominant deciding value of *evidence*. They can get products and services from lots of different people, but usually their strongest deciding value of evidence is the first bridge any sales or service person will need to build.

Reserved style people will want to see proof and validation about what you're saying – facts versus opinions – before they worry about price, enjoyment, ego or being put at ease.

Using the Five Es of Buying

Economics, enjoyment, ego, ease and, of course, evidence. Keep these five words strongly held in your mind, especially when you talk about your products and services. Remember, people go through a hierarchy of dominant deciding values.

How well do you structure your customer presentations or recommendations to match the dominant deciding values of people? Or do you just go through features and benefits of the product or service as displayed in a brochure?

Features, benefits and value

Successful business relationships require more than just understanding customer communication styles. People *don't* buy products and services from you ... they don't!

When people buy, they buy what the product or service will do for them – the end-result benefits.

When people agree with you, they do so because you have presented something in terms that are meaningful to them.

Here's an activity to complete that will help you think about how you can show value. Make a note of the name of one of your products or services. Divide the page into three columns and in the first column list all the features you can think of.

Features: A feature is something physical about the product, or something you provide with the service. For example, if you were selling a watch, the leather band would be a feature. If you were selling a financial plan, offering a regular financial and lifestyle review meeting is a feature.

The 'So what?' test

When you have finished listing features, in the next column list the end-result benefits that the customer will receive from each feature.

The adage 'Features tell and benefits sell' is flawed. It's not always the case that every benefit will be of value to a customer.

Here's where you get to apply the 'So what?' test.

This test is a preparation tool that helps you convert your features into more meaningful benefits for customers. Think about a feature of your product and then challenge yourself to convert it to a benefit by asking yourself, "So what? What will this do for the customer?"

Benefits: A benefit is what a physical thing about the product will do for the customer, or what you provide with the service will actually do for the customer.

For example, one benefit of a leather watchband could be its durability. A benefit of the regular financial and lifestyle review meeting would be that customers would receive guidance or reassurance that they are still working toward achieving their financial and lifestyle goals.

Finally, in the last column, think about which of the five dominant deciding values each benefit is likely to appeal to - economics, enjoyment, ego, ease or evidence.

For example, the leather watchband benefit was durability, which might appeal to the dominant deciding value of putting people at ease. The guidance or reassurance that the client receives from the financial planning review meeting would appeal to the dominant deciding value of enjoyment - they might be looking forward to the chat with the financial planner, or they enjoy their lifestyle goals. It also could appeal to putting them at ease - knowing they are still on track toward achieving their goals.

Now, the key point here is that some of the benefits may or may not be of value to the customer. For example, the leather watch band is a feature, and one benefit may be durability, which might put them at ease in some way. But what if the client is more interested in the look, feel and colour of the leather band? Durability may not be so important, and the danger is to talk about the durability of the leather band as opposed to what's most important to the customer - the choice of colour and texture, and the impression (appealing to enjoyment and ego) it will make with their friends, family and business associates.

Again, that's when asking questions provides you with information on which benefits and which features will be most important or of most value to the customer.

Putting it all together

Now you have the key ingredients to complete this important Show value step.

It works like this: If you have asked great questions, the customer will have identified to you what benefits they are seeking (needs and wants are benefits – not features).

Knowing what benefits they are seeking, you now can show real value by explaining how the features of your products and services will deliver the value and benefits they are seeking.

It puts the communication about the value of your products and services into a simple system for both you and your customer.

When you start to implement the action principles, you will be able to build the following key points into your communication with customers:

- Tailor your presentations to Show value to each person's communication style. Remember, people buy for *their* reasons, not yours.
- Features are what a product or service is comprised of. Benefits are what those features will deliver to the customer.
- People have five dominant deciding values: economics, enjoyment, ego, ease and evidence. Ensure you're presenting to their dominant deciding values.
- The second buying fear of a customer is just before they make a buying decision. Their fear is, "Will what I am about to buy really achieve what I want it to?" "Will it be a good decision?" As you're presenting the value you can create for customers, remember to validate your claims with testimonials, evidence and other ways to make the customers comfortable with making a buying decision.

- Actively link your presentation back to the answers you received in the Ask questions step. Use linking statements to Show value to the client, by demonstrating how the features of your products will achieve the benefits they told you they were seeking, or will solve the problems they have.
- Just make sure you're not doing all of the talking. Constantly ask for their feedback and opinions about what you are presenting. Ask them if you are covering the kinds of things they need to know. Do you need to cover something that you're not covering? Keep them involved – because you can't Show value if you're not sure that you're on the right track.
- Highly successful sales and service people know you can't manipulate people into buying – or that if you try, word will get out and not only won't you get repeat or referral business, your reputation will speak loudly that you're not the kind of person customers want to do business with.
- Learning about buyer communication styles is more about understanding that people are different, and we need to respect those differences. Tricky scripts or one-liners aimed at people with certain behaviour or communication styles will surely set you up for failure.

Take a moment now to complete the self-assessment for the Show value step in the Building Customer Trust process.

Circle a number from 1 – 5 to indicate your personal rating for each statement. Rating Key: 1 = Never, 2 = Rarely, 3 = Occasionally, 4 = Often, 5 = Always

Show value:

All of my customer presentations address the specific needs and wants of my customers	1	2	3	4	5
My presentations focus on the value my customers seek from my products and services	1	2	3	4	5
I am skilled at converting product or service features into meaningful customer value	1	2	3	4	5
I always link features and benefits back to the prioritised needs of my customers	1	2	3	4	5
My presentations always consider the dominant deciding values of my customers	1	2	3	4	5
My presentations always reflect the real reasons why customers buy	1	2	3	4	5
My presentations differentiate my products and services from my competitors	1	2	3	4	5
Every customer presentation I make is specifically tailored to the customer	1	2	3	4	5
I understand and articulate the reasons why a customer should buy from me	1	2	3	4	5
I know that what I provide my customers with, they will not get from my competitor	1	2	3	4	5

Interpretation and Action Planning

The higher your score, the more likely this area is one of your strengths. To start a personal development action plan, look to the area(s) where you have rated yourself higher and set a goal(s) to build on that strength. Where you have rated yourself lower, set a goal(s) to improve in some way.

CHAPTER SUMMARY

- ‣ Prioritise your customers' wants and needs and start with the highest priority
- ‣ Use the Five E's of Buying to determine what's motivating your customer's buying decision (Economics, Ego, Enjoyment, Evidence, Ease)
- ‣ People buy for *their* reasons, not for yours
- ‣ Tailor every presentation of your products or service to each customer's individual circumstances

7

Managing customers' obstacles and objections to buying

IT MAY HAPPEN that what you're presenting or recommending to the customer causes them to disagree or raise an obstacle or an objection. However, when you have a clear, genuine and positive intention to make life better for them in some way, in most cases you'll be able to collaboratively work with your customer to effectively manage those obstacles and objections.

For many sales or service people adopting more traditional sales approaches, there's a major flaw in their approach to managing buyer obstacles and objections.

Most obstacles or objections are typically raised by the customer while the sales or service person is presenting their recommended products, services, advice or solutions. In other words, the sales or service person has presented something to the customer that they either don't like, don't agree with or don't want.

This means the sales or service person has to try and overcome the obstacle or objection raised by the customer. The sales or service person is now in the position of needing to defend what they're presenting; they're now required to defend their value. This makes the selling and buying process quite adversarial.

However, the Building Customer Trust process fixes that.

When you complete a thorough fact-find in the Ask questions step, you will avoid most of the typical obstacles and objections your customers might have to buying. Why? Because you would have discovered what's important to the customer about their specific situation. By proactively identifying the likes, dislikes, problems, experiences or issues about the customer's specific situation before you actually present your product, service or advice recommendation, you will reduce the number of potential obstacles and objections raised.

This is one of the most important principles of success for any sales or service person to realise.

It also is what distinguishes the Building Customer Trust process from more traditional and combatant approaches to selling, where the idea is to present product or service features and benefits, and then handle any obstacles as they are raised by the customer.

If you haven't proactively identified potential buyer obstacles and objections through Asking value-discovery questions, the buying and selling experience becomes an endless bout of negotiation, which is more difficult and uncomfortable for both customer and sales or service person.

If you've completed the Build trust, Ask questions and Show value steps as outlined in the blueprint of the Building Customer Trust process, you've presented your products, services, features and benefits in ways that match your customer's specific and individual situation.

This means the Identify obstacles step has already been completed during the Ask questions step.

However, the Identify obstacles step is still placed in the Building

Customer Trust process following the Show value step, so that you recognise the importance of not attempting to move to Confirm the next steps until you're confident and comfortable that you've proactively identified and managed any potential obstacle or objection your customer might have.

In fact, the obstacles and objections at this stage in the process will not actually be identified by the sales or service person ... they will be raised by the customer because the sales or service person hasn't Shown value – they've done a poor job in Asking questions (or have ignored the answers the customer has provided) and simply presented products and service features and benefits that haven't been tailored to the customer's situation.

So, the objective of the Identify obstacles step is to *proactively* determine and remove reasons that might prevent customers from doing business with you. And again, this is completed in the Ask questions and Show value steps.

To help you implement and achieve this objective, here are three action principles for you to consider:

1. Openly invite feedback to determine all obstacles or objections
2. Clarify your understanding
3. Provide solutions with confidence.

Using the Building Customer Trust process isn't always going to result in you identifying and being able to proactively manage all obstacles or objections by your customers. There's no such thing as a 100 percent guarantee of success when using a process dealing with human behaviour.

However, you can be confident that using the Building Customer Trust process will help you identify and manage more potential customer obstacles and objections than if you reverted to more traditional forms of customer engagement, communication and selling.

There is no such thing as
a 100 percent guarantee
of success when using
a process dealing with
human behaviour.

For that reason, if you are faced with needing to reactively manage a buyer obstacle or objection you will need to know how to effectively do so.

As you've read several times in this book, People Get Your Truth! Over time, your intentions, promises, actions and results will either promote you as trustworthy or expose you as untrustworthy.

This is especially true when you find you've somehow missed identifying an obstacle or objection of a customer and the customer raises an issue with what you're presenting or recommending to them.

Dealing with these issues should never be a game of you versus them.

Rather, you need to see it as an opportunity to live up to your positive intention for the customer. It's not easy when a potential buyer raises a barrier that could prevent the sale from being achieved. However, remember it's not an attack on you personally (well, in most situations, we hope), but there's something about what you've presented that needs to be dealt with before the customer will make the purchase.

This is where you need skill to ask questions, clarify your understanding and listen, to ensure you identify what the real issue or obstacle is, and then use your intentional action to structure an appropriate response.

One way to validate what you are saying when dealing with the obstacle or objection is to use examples of other customers' experiences to overcome the objection.

It's also important to remember that the only issue or obstacle you can never solve is one you don't know about. (This doesn't mean you will always be able to solve your client's issues or obstacles.)

Henry Ford was quoted as saying, "If there is any one secret of success, it lies in the ability to get the other person's point of view, and see things from that person's angle as well as from your own."

This is a great reminder that you are trying to create an environment where customers feel comfortable and confident they're making a wise buying decision. You need to see things from their point of view, acknowledge their point of view, and remember the only way to overcome an obstacle or objection is to first truly understand what it is, and whether you can do anything about it.

Seek feedback often

Sometimes customers will readily raise obstacles or objections to buying, or tell you about issues they have with what you are presenting to them. However, sometimes you need to check if there are any problems that you haven't satisfactorily covered during your Show value step.

Asking feedback questions helps to uncover problems or obstacles. Some examples are:

- How do you feel about this?
- How do you think this would work for you?
- Am I covering what you are looking for?

When asked feedback questions, your customers will clarify any issues you haven't covered, or concerns they still may have, or questions they still need to resolve before they are ready to think about a buying decision.

As a professional sales or service person, the way you handle customer issues, concerns, obstacles and objections will be a significant step toward distancing you from your competitors.

Here's an exercise to help you proactively and confidently handle most objections that will come your way.

The first step is to list any obstacles and objections you have personally encountered that have potentially prevented a customer from proceeding with a purchase. Also, list those you haven't encountered but think you might at some stage (even though you hope you never will).

Most objections raised by
the customer when you're
presenting a recommended
product or service are
the fault of a poor
communication process.

The second step is to write out what you would say and do to deal with each of the obstacles or objections.

Step three is, for those that you struggle to find an answer for, to find other sales or service people who you respect and ask for their feedback on how they would deal with the obstacle or objection.

This activity, when completed and revisited regularly, will help prepare you to comfortably and confidently handle obstacles and objections.

This is not an exercise to develop off-the-shelf or generic responses that sound like you've practised them repeatedly – that's script-based selling. What I'm suggesting is that the more you are prepared, the better you will be able to structure an appropriate response, depending on who is raising the obstacle or objection.

Whenever an issue, obstacle or objection is identified, there are two key principles to apply when you respond.

Step 1 – recognition: Make sure the customer knows you have heard the objection; that you realise it is a real concern for them; and that you understand what they are saying. If you don't understand their concern, ask for more clarification. Remember, this is your opportunity to be truly customer focused and live up to your positive intention for your customer.

Step 2 –reassurance: Explain to the customer how you will deal with the issue, obstacle or objection. If possible, use past experiences in which you have been able to effectively deal with the issue for other customers.

What about price?

It may also be that after discussing possible solutions you find that the product or service you are offering, at the price you are offering it, seems to be a problem for the customer.

Clients will have a problem with your price only for two reasons:

Reason 1: They simply can't afford what you are offering at the price you need to charge.

This is a difficult situation and one where many sales or service people struggle. If the customer can't afford what you are offering, your immediate response may be to discount.

Be careful! Once you discount your products or services you are undervaluing their worth immediately. More than this: discount once for the customer and they may always expect the same discount level (maybe with other products and services), and may tell their associates and friends about the discounted price they paid.

You need to be very aware at what point discounting your products or services no longer mean profitable sales. Anyone can sell anything once. All you need to be is the cheapest!

Reason 2: They can afford it but simply don't see the value at the price you are charging. This objection simply takes you back to being able to show how your products and services will create the value your customers expect.

There are no magic formulas for overcoming price objections, but your ability to handle them is a direct reflection on your belief in the value your product or service will create for your customer.

There are several strategies you can adopt in dealing with a price objection. Your choice will depend on the situation. Here are just a few you might reword and adapt to suit your personality and style:

- Come up with an effective repayment plan (so they can afford it over time).
- Restructure the offer to reduce the features/benefits (and therefore price) to enable them to afford it.
- Demonstrate better why your products or service are priced to create the most value for your customer, and that the value they receive is worth the price they will pay.
- Refer them to a cheaper alternative.
- As a last resort, bearing in mind all that has been said about discounting, you might decide to take the hit and offer a discount. Just be aware of the consequences.

Highly successful sales and service people understand that not every customer will want what you sell. There are nearly always alternatives. However, the more you believe in the value you create at the price you charge, and in how you differentiate from your competitors, the easier it will be to handle issues, obstacles and objections.

The key message in this chapter is that when you apply the Building Customer Trust process, you're applying a customer-engagement and trust-building process that is driven by a positive intention for your customers, and will allow you in most cases to proactively identify potential obstacles or objections before they are raised by the customer.

In this way you can then adjust and tailor your presentation and recommendations of products, services or advice by selecting only those features and benefits that will be of meaningful value to the customer.

Twenty most common buyer obstacles and objections

Here are 20 of the most common buyer obstacles and objections that you may encounter if you haven't completed the Ask questions step and adjusted your Show value step in the Building Customer Trust process.

If you do unfortunately find yourself in that situation and need to reactively, rather than proactively, manage and overcome an obstacle or objection, the following tips will be of assistance.

Please understand, I'm not recommending you learn and use these tips as sure-fire scripts to reactively overcome any buyer obstacle or objection. I'm also not claiming that if you use these tips they will be effective for you. While these are all legitimate ways that successful sales and service people have overcome and managed the obstacle or objection being discussed, your specific circumstances and contexts may be different.

Your intention and belief in the value you provide when you sell what you sell becomes very clear when a customer raises an objection.

1. "I need time to think about it."

Some customers really do need time to think about whether they want to proceed or not with their purchase. It's not really an obstacle or objection that will prevent them from buying, it's just that they genuinely need time to think about it.

Here are two strategies you will find effective:

Strategy (1): Let them know you're happy for them to take time to think about it and that in fact you'd encourage them to do so. But also, let them know you've given them all the information you can, based on what they've told you they're after, to help them make a good decision. Finally, make sure that you provide a 'call to action' by suggesting a time in your diary (allowing enough time for them to think about their decision) and lock in another appointment, phone call, etc.

Strategy (2): Alternatively, while still letting them know you're happy for them to take time to think about it and that in fact you'd encourage them to do so, add a question like, "I just want to make sure that I've done my job properly before you leave to think about it, so I wonder if there's anything I haven't covered, or any information that you still need, or any concerns that you still have to help you in your decision process?" Depending on their answer, you'd again finish with a 'call to action' by suggesting a time in your diary (allowing enough time for them to think about their decision) and lock in another appointment, phone call, etc.

2. I want to shop around."

This is like the previous obstacle where the customer says they need time to think about it. Some customers, as part of their buying decision process, like to shop around to make sure that they're about to make a wise buying decision. If you've done your job properly, be confident that if they shop around they will come back to you because you have really listened to what they need and have tailored a solution that will best fulfil the value they are seeking.

Use the tips in the previous obstacle discussion to help here.

3. "You're too expensive."

The easier and more common person response here is to discount until you get the sale. However, as you've already read, discounting should always be a last resort. There are only two reasons why people believe your price is too expensive (everything will fit into one of these two reasons):

The first is that they just can't afford it, and the second is that they don't see the value in what you're offering at the price you're offering it.

If they can't afford it, maybe they can afford it under different payment options. If you have the flexibility of being creative with your payment terms, see if you can come to some arrangement on the how and when they can pay. A word of caution here, though: make sure that you don't adversely affect your cash flow and/or the payment terms of other customers you're dealing with.

If they don't see the value, what you need to do is to once again stack up the value units to equal the price. You do this by repeating what the customer has said they're after and how what you will do for them will deliver that value. One option here is to say to the customer something like, "This is what you've said you're after, and this is what we can do for you to make sure that you receive just that. If we're too expensive, which of what you're after don't you want?"

This is not a strategy in being smart or arrogant, it's simply letting the customer know that these are the terms that you need to do business.

Another strategy, if they say that you're too expensive, is to say something like, "Sure, we're not cheap, but our pricing reflects the quality that you will receive, and we guarantee (if you do) that you will receive that quality you've told us you're seeking. So, other than price at this stage, is there anything else we need to discuss before we proceed?" This approach opens the customer up to the opportunity of letting you know if there's something other than price that they need for you to deal with before they proceed.

It's not what you sell ...

It's how and why you sell it!

Yet another strategy is to say something like, "We know that all of our customers want the best price possible, and I want to assure you that the price I've quoted you will best allow us to deliver the quality and value you've told us you're seeking."

The key here is that you don't want to get into a commodity-based pricing war. If they come back to you with a cheaper price from a competitor, don't be too ready to discount – if you do, you're now in the commodity pricing game, and the cheapest price wins ... but at what cost to the long-term success of the business?

Distance yourself from the price of your competitors by doing a great customer interview in the Ask questions step of the Building Customer Trust process and uncover exactly what the customer is looking for and structuring your presentation to those specific situations of your customers.

This may not always win you the "You're too expensive" sale, but it will certainly move you closer to winning more than you will lose.

A *note on proactive discounting.* Proactive discounting is a process where you let the customer know the standard pricing structure for what you're offering, and then you provide them with a reason (for example volume, repeat business opportunities or other special circumstances) that allows you to discount the price. You then let them know that this is your best price (and stick to it).

The key to this strategy is you've discounted before the customer has asked you to do so, thereby not reactively defending your value.

4. "There are too many features I don't need."

If a customer raises this as an obstacle or objection you've not completed your Building Customer Trust process very well! What they are telling you is, you are *capability focused* and not intentionally customer focused.

If you flood the customer with all the features and all the benefits of your products or service, there's the danger that they'll say: "Well, you're too expensive and there's too many added extras I'm paying for that I don't really want or need."

To deal with this, you're best to take the customer back to the Ask questions stage and admit that maybe you've misunderstood exactly what they're after, by saying something like, "OK, maybe I've missed exactly what you're after. Let me ask you a couple of questions to make sure I understand."

This enables you to at least try to salvage a potential loss of sale by letting the customer know that you want to make sure you provide the best solution for them.

The key here is to ask questions to help determine whether the customer does have a need for the additional features and benefits that you presented, which then takes the additional information from being capability driven to more customer focused.

5. "I have a preferred supplier (I'd rather deal with someone else)."

This is a tough one, and the reality is, you'd hope your own customers would be saying this to your competitors. However, one strategy to deal with this is to let the customer know that you respect that relationship that they have with your competitor, and what you're not trying to do is undermine that relationship.

Let the customer know you are trying to discuss ways you might be able to add further value to what they're already achieving with their existing supplier. And you then pursue the conversation with some questions that will gauge whether there are opportunities for you to add value to create an even better solution for the customer than they are already experiencing.

6. "I'm not sure about your company's reputation."

This is one of those obstacles and objections that should never be raised by the customer. Rather, it should have been discovered earlier in the conversation through questions about companies they respect, have heard good things about, have bought from in the past, and what they expect from a company or brand when they buy something.

In most instances when customers raise objections to your recommendations it means you need to revisit the Ask questions step.

However, if you haven't uncovered this earlier in your Building Customer Trust process, then one appropriate response is to get the customer to articulate what you should have found out earlier. Try something like: "What is it about our reputation that is of concern?"

If there have been some problems that your company has had in the past, don't sweep them under the rug – admit them, but then get the customer focused on the future and how you can help them achieve their goals, despite the history of the problem existing.

Try something like: "You're right, we've had some problems with that in the past, and we've been working hard to fix it. In fact, if you were to ask our customers now how they're going with experiencing that kind of problem, I know you will find nothing but glowing reports." (You could only say something like this if it's true.)

Another strategy is to turn the customer's concern about your company's reputation into a positive by saying something like, "You're right, we've had some problems with that in the past, and we've been working hard to fix it. I'm just wondering, if we could fix that specific problem, is there anything else we would need to do before we could proceed and do business together?"

7. **"I've had a bad experience with your company (or have heard of others who have had a bad experience with you company)."**

This is similar to obstacle 6 – "I'm not sure about your company's reputation", and the tips in that section will be of value to you.

8. **"I don't see the value in what you're offering."**

This is an interesting one and suggests you may not have fully uncovered or understood exactly what the customer was looking for and have either undersold or oversold the value by not tailoring your presentation to the specific needs, wants and situation of the customer. In other words, you may have sold your capability and not value.

An objection raised by a customer is not usually a personal attack on you ... unless you've let your ego get in the way and put trust at risk.

If a customer says, "I don't see the value" you need to go back to the Ask questions step in your Building Customer Trust process by asking something like, "Well, maybe I've misunderstood what you're looking for. As I understood it, these were the key things you're trying to achieve with this purchase (and you would outline the key needs, wants or problems that the customer has outlined to you). Other than these, what else is important to you and that you're trying to achieve?"

This type of response is trying to get the customer to reveal any uncovered or unstated issues that you will need to address in your presentation of the value you can create through the product or service that you're offering.

9. "I'm worried about the quality and whether I will receive what you're promising."

This type of response is rarely said out loud, but may be inside a buyer's head when they haven't received enough validation or evidence that you can deliver on your promises.

However, if a customer does say something like this, you might want to respond with, "I'm pretty sure I've understood what you're looking for, so what I've got to be able to do now is validate to you that we can deliver on what it is I've said we can do. Let me ask you, what is it that I haven't been able to show you or explain to you so far, that's causing you to worry about whether it will do what we've been discussing?"

This puts the ball back into the customer's court to help you to understand what it will take for them to feel confident in the quality and delivery of the value they are seeking.

10. "Where's the proof or evidence this will do what you're saying it will?"

Your response to this obstacle is similar to the previous one regarding quality.

11. "I need to refer my decision to someone else."

This again should be an obstacle that was identified well before you got into any presentation of your products or services. During the Ask questions step in your Building Customer Trust process, a question you would typically ask is something like, "When you're making a buying decision on purchases like this, is there anyone else who you would typically involve so that you feel confident you're making the right decision?"

However, if the customer springs this on you when you're trying to find out if they're ready to make a buying decision, you could respond with something like, "I'm happy for you to refer to (the person) because I want to make sure you're confident you're making the best choice. What I'd like to recommend is that you and (the other person) meet with me and we can all discuss what needs to happen to make sure you get exactly what you're looking for. How's Tuesday next week at 9 o'clock (or whatever the appropriate time is)?"

Here's another example, "I'm happy for you refer to (the person) because I want you to be confident you're making the best choice. Before you do that, though, I want to make sure I've done my job properly. Is there anything I haven't shown or explained to you that we still need to cover, that's going to help you in your discussions with (the person)?"

12. "The service terms and conditions don't meet my needs."

The key with this type of obstacle is to ensure, before you start to work through any negotiation on the terms, that you're confident the potential customer wants what you're selling.

You might start by asking something like, "OK, so the terms are something we'll need to work on, but if we can sort these terms out, is there anything else we would need to cover before we can proceed?"

What this does is check that the terms are the problem and not something else. If the answer is in the affirmative – that they'd be

The way you manage customer objections often holds the key to future repeat or referral sales.

happy to buy if you can sort out the terms – it then just gets down to whether you've got any flexibility in the way your terms can be structured.

13. "I like your competitor's product (or service) better."

Ouch! The potential buyer is now letting you know that they've shopped around. Your objective here is not to do battle against the competitor's product, but to restate how your product or service can best meet the needs and wants that you've uncovered.

You might try something like, "I want to make sure that you get the best value you can from making this purchase ... and I don't want to sell you something that you're not going to be absolutely delighted with. The reality is that all the products (or services) in the market can pretty much do the basics of what you're after; however, based on what you've told me, the three key things that you're looking for above and beyond just the basic outcomes you'd expect from something like this are (and you'd point out the key areas that your product will do better than your competitors'). And I'm sure if you compare what we can do with those key points in mind, you'll find that what I'm recommending is the best solution for you. Can you see how these areas will be a better solution for you?"

If they say Yes, then you're on your way forward and you can say something like, "Then the next steps for us are ..." and you outline what the next steps are for the purchase to be made.

If they say No, then the reality is, they've probably made their decision to buy your competitor's product. You might like to try another strategy by saying something like, "OK. I can see that you really like our competitor's product (or service), but I just want to make sure I've done my best for you. Is there anything I could do that would cause you to choose my product over the competitor's product?"

If they respond with something that you could do, you're back in the sale. If they respond with something that you can't do, let it go; but wish them well and remind them that you're happy to help them in the future.

14. "I don't understand the fees or terms and conditions."

This really is simply a clarifying exercise that requires you to ask a question and then to deal with whatever the confusion is. Ask something like, "I've probably not explained things as well as I could. Let me see if I can fix that. What is it specifically about our terms or fees that you'd like me to go over with you?" Then deal with each issue as appropriate.

15. "What if you leave and things go wrong?"

This is an obstacle of future concern that is often raised, either internally in the customer's thoughts or externally when they voice their concern to you. What they're concerned about is whether the value they are seeking will continue if you happen to leave.

This requires you to put your ego to one side and not just sell you and the product or service, but to sell your company, the product and service and, where appropriate, sell a process not a product or service.

Provide your customers with the name of someone you recommend within your company for them to contact should for any reason they not be able to contact you personally.

16. "There's no real difference between yours or your competitors' products or services."

This is similar to obstacle 13 and you could structure your responses similarly to those outlined there.

17. "I'm not sure I want to do business with you."

This is never easy – for some reason some people will find something about you that causes them concern – thank goodness this is more of an exception than a rule. Depending on the type of business you're in, here are a couple of strategies you might like to consider.

Separate yourself from the sale – sell the process or outcome and not you. For example, if it's your age that's the problem (too old or too young), you might respond with something like, "I know that

How convinced are you of the value you provide when you sell what you sell?

sometimes the age of a salesperson can be of concern, but in this case, what we're offering has little to do with my age. I want to make sure that I provide the best outcome for you, so let's just go over again exactly what it is that you're looking for." This will help to get the buyer focused back on the purchase and off you as an individual.

Another way to separate you from the sale is to focus on your company's belief and trust in you. For example, you might say something like, "I'm sorry you feel that way about dealing specifically with me. Our company has selected the sales and service team based on the skills and knowledge that they know will enable us to offer the best value to our customers. I want to make sure that I can prove to you that, despite your concern, I can deliver what you're after. So just for now, could we go over what it is that you're specifically looking for, let me show you what we can do to help you, and then you can let me know if you want to proceed or not?"

Another strategy, if the above doesn't work, can be to ask if they'd like to see another sales or service representative (if appropriate).

18. "I'm not sure I need it just yet."

This is only an 'obstacle in time'. Keep in mind the reality may be that they really don't need it just yet. The customer hopefully has said Yes, they like what you're offering, they're now simply saying, "But not just right now". Here are a couple of strategies, depending on the situation:

Refer the customer back to what they've said they're trying to achieve and point out how even though the priority might not be high right now, if they were to purchase the product or service now, the outcomes they would achieve and the value they would receive will be delivered

Ask something like, "I don't want to push you into buying something you don't want. What I do want to make sure of, though, is that the goals you've outlined to me are realised. If it was possible for you to buy our product (or service), what would need to be in place that is currently not?"

Another strategy is to get a commitment of when they might be ready to buy.

19. "You're selling me this one because you're on a better commission if you do."

If this is true, then you don't deserve to win the sale. If it's not, you have probably focused too much on the product (or service) and not enough on showing how what the customer is after can be best achieved by your recommended product or service.

You might try responding with something like, "My job isn't just to sell you any product – it's to try and best understand exactly what you're after, and then to present to you what I believe to be the best solution I can offer. What you've told me is that these are the things you're trying to achieve (go over the needs they've identified for you, seeking feedback that you've got them right), and the reason I'm recommending this particular product (or service) is (explain how this product will best achieve the outcomes they are seeking)."

20. "I'll get back to you."

This is like an objection 1: "I need time to think about it ". Your responses could be similar to those recommended for that obstacle.

It's all about intention

Whether you like or even agree with the above tips on how to reactively deal with the 20 most common buyer obstacles or objections, what's inescapable in its truth is that when customers raise obstacles or objections to what you're recommending they buy, however you respond, your customers will be looking through a window to your truth.

That's why being mindfully aware of your positive intention for each customer (what you want them to have or experience) is the foundation upon which you will be able to make intentional promises on what you can and can't deliver in terms of features, benefits and tailored value. This is how you can earn the trust of your customers. This is what will earn you the sales results you expect and want. This is the real power of the Building Customer Trust process.

Your self-assessment for the Identify obstacles step is provided on the following page.

Circle a number from 1 – 5 to indicate your personal rating for each statement. Rating Key: 1 = Never, 2 = Rarely, 3 = Occasionally, 4 = Often, 5 = Always					
Identify obstacles:					
I react well to obstacles, issues, objections or challenges raised by the customer	1	2	3	4	5
I keep my ego controlled when obstacles are raised by customers	1	2	3	4	5
I accept that customers have the right to question or challenge what I say	1	2	3	4	5
I know why customers might have obstacles or objections to what's being presented in a customer meeting	1	2	3	4	5
I can handle any obstacle or objection raised during a customer meeting	1	2	3	4	5
I can demonstrate my true points of differentiation from my competitors	1	2	3	4	5
I know how to tailor my points of differentiation for every customer	1	2	3	4	5
I am confident in how I handle challenges on the price or fees I charge	1	2	3	4	5
I know when a negotiated opportunity with a customer is a win-win situation	1	2	3	4	5
I use discounting only ever as a strategy of last resort	1	2	3	4	5

Interpretation and Action Planning

The higher your score, the more likely this area is one of your strengths. To start a personal development action plan, look to the area(s) where you have rated yourself higher and set a goal(s) to build on that strength. Where you have rated yourself lower, set a goal(s) to improve in some way.

CHAPTER SUMMARY

▸ Most obstacles or objections raised by customers are the result of a poor communication process

▸ Ask better questions to proactively identify and manage potential obstacles or issues before they're raised by the customer

▸ When reactively managing obstacles or objections, keep your customer intention at top of mind

▸ A tailored Show value step will usually eliminate most obstacles or objections to buying

8

Confirm next steps

TYPICALLY, THIS STEP in a sales system is referred to as *closing the sale*, but not in the Building Customer Trust process. Closing sounds like an end-point; but when a customer buys, it's not the end – it's the beginning of them validating they've made a wise decision to buy from you.

This is what can make all the difference in your long-term success in business sales and service.

When you confirm the next steps with a customer, it's the start of you proving you can deliver what you've promised. It's the start of the customer receiving and enjoying the value you have intentionally promised.

So, don't close sales!

Confirm the next steps by recommending and agreeing what the next steps will be in your experience with the customer.

The objective of this step is to gain confirmation to take the appropriate next steps to commence or continue the business relationship. The action principles to implement the objective of this step are to:

1. Reinforce the value they will receive
2. Ask the checkpoint question
3. Confirm the next appropriate steps for you and the customer.

Most sales training and how-to-sell books tend to focus on this step more than any other. There are many books written specifically on ways to close sales. Here are just a few better-known and often-referred-to closing techniques you may have heard of:

- The intimidator close
- The believer's close
- The make 'em feel guilty close
- The get 'em smiling close
- The fear of loss close
- The answer for everything close
- The puppy dog close
- The hat in hand close
- The slip up on 'em when they're not looking and kick 'em in the kidney close.

Each of these closing techniques uses communication, influencing and persuasion strategies that set up and put pressure on the customer to say yes and buy, and I'm certainly not going to distract you from a more intentional and integrity-based approach to Building Customer Trust by discussing them in any detail here.

Here's where the Building Customer Trust process differs from most other sales and customer engagement strategies. When you confirm the next steps, you're helping the customer to comfortably and confidently arrive at a buying decision. Said another way, you confidently recommend the next steps for the customer to receive the value they seek.

The right time to confirm next steps

The right time to confirm next steps is when you've successfully completed all the previous steps in the Building Customer Trust process. What that means is:

- You are clear on your positive intention to make life better in some way for the customer.
- You have built trust and gained a level of rapport with the customer.
- You have asked questions to assist both you and the customer to better understand exactly what they need.
- You have shown value in how your products and services will meet the specific and tailored needs and expectations of your customer.
- You have identified obstacles before the client has raised them and have tailored your presentation in the Show value step to allow for those potential obstacles or objections. Or you have been able to reactively manage and overcome any identified obstacles and objections when customers have raised them.

You see, if you have been able to do all that, what is there left to do but to simply confirm next steps?

That's why the Building Customer Trust process is just that – a process. If you successfully complete each step, it moves both you and the customer towards a natural, comfortable and reciprocal decision that the customer will buy.

What this means is the time to confirm next steps is when you are sure the customer is ready to proceed with their purchase. But how do you know if the customer is ready to buy? One way is to constantly seek the customer's opinions and feedback throughout your discussion with them. You'll remember this is one of the action principles in the Show value step.

This is one of the most important communication principles to learn – not just in sales, but in life. Constantly seek people's feedback

Don't flood your customers with all the information you want to present. Seek their feedback often.

on what you are saying, what you are presenting and what you are suggesting. Use feedback and opinion-based questions like, "How do you feel about this?" and "Am I covering the things you want to hear about?"

However, the key is to seek feedback incrementally.

Don't wait until you've presented everything you want to cover to help the customer make a wise buying decision. Check in with them as you discuss each key point, feature, benefit and value.

The checkpoint question

Here's a checkpoint question to help you determine whether you've completed all the steps in the Building Customer Trust process:

Other than what we've covered so far, is there anything else we need to look at before we (proceed)?

You can see I've put the word proceed in brackets. That's because you can replace it with whatever you believe the next appropriate action is for you to deliver the value for the client ... in other words for them to confirm next steps with you.

When you ask a checkpoint question like this, when you believe you've completed all the steps in the Building Customer Trust process, if there is something else they would like to discuss or discover, simply go back to the Ask questions step and then cover the topic by moving through the Building Customer Trust process.

In response to your checkpoint question, if the client tells you there is nothing else they want to cover, you simply confirm the next appropriate steps for them to receive the value they seek.

How you do that will depend on the product or service you are providing. It could be starting the paperwork for the order. It could be confirming a start date. It could be preparing a formal proposal on what has just been agreed. It could be wrapping up the product and using the client's credit card. This is why it's referred to as 'Confirm next steps' and not 'Close the sale'. It's confirming whatever the next appropriate steps are for the customer to receive the value they seek. It's not pushing them to decide ... it's not closing the sale. In fact, it's linking the next step in the process, which is to stay in touch to deliver on the value.

Remember our earlier discussion on the three buyer exit ramps. Each ramp is a question clients potentially ask along their buyer's journey. The first buyer exit ramp is the Initial Contact ramp and the customer asks this question of themselves, "What's this buying experience going to be like?"

Throughout this book we've been discussing how to overcome this first buyer exit ramp. We've covered the importance of getting clear on what your intention is for your customer – what you want *for* them, not what you want from them. By setting a clear intention to make their life better in some way helps you become more intentionally in the moment when you're with the customer. It helps them get your truth and to fast-track trust. It helps them get comfortable with their buying experience with you. It helps them remove their first buyer exit ramp and continue their buyer's journey with you.

The second buyer exit ramp is the Decision Point exit ramp and customers ask this question silently to themselves, "This all sounds good, but if I say yes, what could go wrong?"

Again, throughout this book we've discussed how to manage and remove this second buyer exit ramp. By setting your positive intention for the customer you've mindfully asked better questions, listened to what the customer's wants and needs are, and have tailored your presentation and recommendations in the Show value step in ways that remove their concerns about what could go wrong.

This then leaves only the third buyer exit ramp for us to manage.

The Post Sale exit ramp is where the customers ask themselves after they've bought from you, "What have I just done? Was it a good decision to buy from you?" How to manage this third buyer exit ramp is the focus of our next chapter.

Here's your self-assessment for the Confirm next steps step.

Circle a number from 1 – 5 to indicate your personal rating for each statement. Rating Key: 1 = Never, 2 = Rarely, 3 = Occasionally, 4 = Often, 5 = Always.

Confirm next steps:

I know how to gauge if the customer is ready to buy	1	2	3	4	5
I ask feedback and opinion questions to help check if I've understood the customer's wants and needs	1	2	3	4	5
I know when to ask the Checkpoint Question	1	2	3	4	5
I'm confident to make recommendations and confirm the next steps	1	2	3	4	5
When confirming the next steps, I am always confident the customer will proceed	1	2	3	4	5
I know how to reduce or remove the second buyer exit ramp (the decision-point fear)	1	2	3	4	5
I strongly believe in the value I can create when customers buy from me	1	2	3	4	5
Our products and services are priced in a way that is competitive	1	2	3	4	5
I know how to reinforce the value a customer will receive before confirming the next steps	1	2	3	4	5
I can clearly state for the customer what the next appropriate action steps are	1	2	3	4	5

Interpretation and Action Planning

The higher your score, the more likely this area is one of your strengths. To start a personal development action plan, look to the area(s) where you have rated yourself higher and set a goal(s) to build on that strength. Where you have rated yourself lower, set a goal(s) to improve in some way,

CHAPTER SUMMARY

‣ Confirming next steps is simply recommending the next appropriate action steps to help the customer experience the value they seek

‣ Neither the customer nor you ought to feel any pressure as you Confirm next steps

‣ You don't need 101 ways to 'close' a sale if you've completed all the previous steps in the Building Customer Trust process

Stay in touch

THE OBJECTIVE OF THE STAY IN TOUCH STEP is to create customer service experiences that reinforce, validate and reward customers, and to earn advocacy. You want customers to become fans of you, your products or service and your business. You want to earn the right for customers to want to buy from you again (where appropriate) and to recommend and refer others to you.

The action principles that will help you achieve this objective are:

1. Thank customers for their business
2. Confirm that the value delivered has met expectations
3. Add extra meaningful value.

As you've just read, closing seems to be the final step in most sales systems, but the Building Customer Trust process strongly suggests that it can't end there for long-term success.

This is one of the most powerful principles, which many sales and service people seem to forget. And it all has to do with the third buyer exit ramp – the after-sale fear. After-sale fear occurs after the customer has bought; and the fear the customer often has is formed into a question they silently ask themselves: "What have I just agreed to? Have I made a good decision? Will I regret this in the future? Did I make the right decision to buy from this person (or this business)?"

Highly effective, professional sales and service people not only understand this third fear of buying, but act upon it by staying in touch with the customer to ensure what they promised is received.

Here are some strategies to reduce this third buyer exit ramp.

Look for ways to 'thank' the customer for their business. You could send an email and hope it cuts through all the other emails the customer receives (and deletes). Or is the investment in a postage stamp with a traditional letter of thanks something you could consider? What about a handwritten card? Make sure your thankyou letters or cards don't go out with the invoice!

Build positive relationships with, and keep close to, the service delivery people who will be looking after your customer after the sale. Help the customer by giving them a contact name and number of a specially assigned customer service contact. If you are the only person involved, make sure you have identified with the customer how they would like to be kept up to date (phone, letter, email, text, etc.).

Continually ask yourself what you might do after the sale has been made to create additional value for the customer – something they didn't expect or have to pay for? This is an important question to answer. Think of ways to say very loudly, "We value your business, and here's something that validates our appreciation of your doing business with us."

Where's my gift basket?

Here's an example of Staying in touch. When we sold our home where we'd lived with our two sons for all of their pre-teenage years, the real estate agent we chose to act on our behalf did a good job. We sold the house prior to auction for an amount we were very happy with. We had purchased a new property through a different agency.

What are you prepared
to do that will create a
'wow' experience for your
customers after they've
bought?

We also liked the style of this other agent, even though he was acting on behalf of the vendor and wasn't really focused on looking after us. All in all, the sale and purchase went smoothly and we were satisfied.

I'm sure that's a fairly typical scenario for most people. However, our new neighbours, soon after we moved in, decided it was time for them to move a little closer to where their two girls went to school (they assured us it had nothing to do with us moving in as their neighbours – just in case you were wondering).

They also had one real estate agent selling their home and a different agent for the purchase of their new home. Neither of these agents were the same ones that we had been involved with.

Bernadette was the name of the agent who sold our neighbours' home. On the day of the auction, with a record above-reserve sale price being achieved, she popped open a bottle of French champagne for our neighbours. No big deal, I hear you say. But wait for the rest of the story.

On the day they moved into their new home, our now ex-neighbours received a beautiful gift basket full of goodies and another bottle of French champagne from Bernadette.

Now remember, Bernadette was not the agent involved in the purchase of their new home, only the sale of their old home.

My question is, "Where's my gift basket?"

I can assure you, when people ask if I know a good real estate agent, I recommend Bernadette.

A surprise in the boot

Here's another example. When I bought a new car quite a few years ago, I drove off the lot feeling very pleased with my purchase. It's always a great feeling to drive a new car, with that new smell and feel about it.

As I turned the first corner, I remember smiling because I thought Slavko (the car salesperson) had pre-set the car stereo – it just happened to be playing my favourite piece of classical music, Pachelbel's Canon. I remember when I first walked into the customer service section of the car dealership it was playing in the background. When I met Slavko, I remember mentioning to him how much I liked that music. Nothing else was said.

As I continued to drive, I realised that it wasn't the radio; it was a CD playing. (Yes ... a CD – it was quite some time ago!) In fact, when I arrived home I found four CDs of some of my favourite classical music in the stacker. Wow – what an impact that made. By the way, I also found a golf umbrella, tees and golf balls in the boot of the car with a personal note saying, "Enjoy the next round ... Regards, Slavko".

Slavko has since moved on from that car dealership, but I have bought my last three cars from them. While I'll always remember this experience, because it was not expected, the sales and service experience I receive from this dealership keeps me wanting to come back.

Now, here's the point. Every car salesperson could do something like that. But they don't. Every real estate agent could do something like Bernadette did. But they don't. Why not? The answer is one of the scourges of modern-day business, known as *after-sale apathy*.

After-sale apathy is what our research has shown as the major cause of lower levels of repeat and referral business. After-sale apathy gives fuel to the third buyer exit ramp. Customers take this ramp when they do not receive any positive, meaningful or value-added after-sale contact by a sales or service person, or do not feel that they are genuinely valued as a customer. They never refer. They never return to buy again.

So, here is a must-answer question for you. What are you doing currently, or could you be doing, to create additional and unexpected value or provide a positive buying experience for your customers after the sale is completed?

How will you thank your clients for choosing to do business with you?

You can learn some great lessons by thinking about your own buying experiences and those of your family and friends when they tell you about their experiences – the good and the bad.

That personal handwritten note

I remember answering a phone call recently from the Epilepsy Association of Australia, seeking a donation for their charity. We get calls and requests from a wide range of charities, some of which we are happy to donate to and some that we choose not to. But the Epilepsy Association of Australia is one charity that we are very quick to say yes to.

It's not because we have any connection with the charity, or even because we know a few people who live with epilepsy. The reason stems from way back, after we made our first donation to that charity. A few days after donating, we received in the mail a typical, computer-generated, standard "Thank you for donating" letter.

I don't remember even reading the letter, but what I did read was this personal handwritten note, on the bottom right-hand corner of the letter. It simply read, "Thank you, Mr and Mrs Penglase, for your kind donation. Regards, Anthony (Volunteer)".

What Anthony the volunteer had achieved was to get my attention and cause me to say, "Wow". I remember saying to my wife, "How simple is that?" Anthony had turned a high-tech letter into a high-touch experience.

Thinking about and then taking some action on these ideas will take your business relationships with customers to a deeper level of satisfaction and trust.

Here's a challenge

1. Over the next few weeks, make a list of all the customers you have forged relationships with over the past three months.

2. Next, answer these questions for each customer:
   - How have I thanked this customer for their business?
   - How did I keep them informed and involved in the after-sales process?
   - What agreed method and regularity of contact has been established?
   - What did I do after the sale was completed to create extra value for this customer – something they didn't expect or pay for?

3. Based on your answers, take some action to reconnect and stay in touch with your customers. It's never too late.

Now, I realise it depends on the type of business and the number of customers you work as to the number of these steps that will be possible for you. However, the more you can do, the better your Stay in touch step will be, and the more repeat and referral business you will earn.

Testimonials, referrals and introductions

Seeking and earning testimonials, referrals and introductions is an important part of the Stay in touch step. Here's a guiding principle about testimonials, referrals and introductions, which is often practised poorly. The principle is that you get valuable testimonials, referrals and introductions when you have earned them.

Unfortunately, in more old-school and traditional sales and customer engagement approaches, sales or service people were taught to ask for testimonials, referrals or introductions straight after closing the sale.

Consider for a moment what it would take for you to recommend one of your friends, a work colleague or a family member to someone else for a business transaction.

Most of your reasons for providing a referral or introduction to a sales or service person will be because of things like trust, quality of the product or service, extra value you've received, the character and integrity of the sales or service person, or value for money.

Now, your reasons may not be exactly the same as what is listed here. However, if you think about your reasons and the ones above, for the most part these will be things you cannot make decisions or form opinions about until after the sale; and more importantly, until after the product or service has been used and experienced by you.

Here's where staying in touch with your customers becomes so important. If you want to reduce the pressure you may feel when asking for a testimonial, referral or introduction, and more importantly, if you want to increase your customers' comfort levels in giving testimonials, referrals or an introduction, wait until they have experienced your products and services!

At that point, because you have kept in touch, ensured they have received what they expected (and wherever possible, exceeded their expectations), asking for a referral, introduction or written testimonial will be a natural continuation of their buying journey.

It's about belief, again

Earning testimonials, referrals or introductions, once again, is more about belief than it is about technique. Think about this for a moment: Why would a sales or service person hesitate or even fear asking for a testimonial, referral or introduction?

The answers are similar to why a sales or service person would be uncomfortable to professionally confirm next steps. That is, they have a fear of failure, don't want to seem pushy, or are not sure if what they have offered or delivered achieves what the customer wants.

Over many years now, and working with a wide range of industries, one of the common messages I hear from customer feedback surveys undertaken by Marketing and Sales departments is that the majority

In sales and customer service you get the new, repeat and referral business you deserve.

of customers would readily provide a testimonial or a referral ... it's just they have never been asked.

It's from this Stay in touch step that your customers will Get Your Truth! It's your intention and belief about what you do that are so important when you stay in touch with your customers. It's in the questions you ask to ensure they are receiving what they expected when they bought. It's in your level of commitment to finding out what else you could do to add even more value to each customer.

Here's the final self-assessment on the Stay in touch step for you to complete.

Circle a number from 1 – 5 to indicate your personal rating for each statement. Rating Key: 1 = Never, 2 = Rarely, 3 = Occasionally, 4 = Often, 5 = Always					
Stay in touch:					
Having confirmed the next steps, I know how to remove the third buyer exit ramp (post-sale fear)	1	2	3	4	5
After the sale, I create additional value the customer doesn't expect or have to pay for	1	2	3	4	5
I always ensure that the value I say will be delivered, gets delivered	1	2	3	4	5
I am staying in touch with new and longstanding customers appropriately	1	2	3	4	5
I always seek introductions, referrals or testimonials from my happy customers	1	2	3	4	5
My customers trust me and know my intention is to deliver exceptional value ... not just get a sale	1	2	3	4	5
I get the number of referrals and introductions to new customers I would like to receive	1	2	3	4	5
I get the number of testimonials I would like to receive	1	2	3	4	5
I have an after-sale stay-in-touch program I implement consistently	1	2	3	4	5
I am achieving the amount of new and repeat business I need to achieve my sales and business goals	1	2	3	4	5

Interpretation and Action Planning

The higher your score, the more likely this area is one of your strengths. To start a personal development action plan, look to the area(s) where you have rated yourself higher and set a goal(s) to build on that strength. Where you have rated yourself lower, set a goal(s) to improve in some way

CHAPTER SUMMARY

- Your intention becomes clear to the customer after the sale has been made
- You earn customer testimonials, referrals and introductions when you meet and where possible exceed expectations
- Your Stay in touch strategies will help you to earn more new, repeat and referral sales

10

A final note from the author

SO, THERE YOU HAVE IT: the Building Customer Trust process. I'm sure by now you feel comfortable and confident in following the objectives and action principles of the process, and you will be more able to create buying environments for your customers to help them become equally confident and comfortable.

When I started to write this book, I was very clear about my intention for you, the reader.

My intention for you is that you discover in these pages, tips and strategies to help you win more new, repeat and referral business. My intention for you is also that you will feel a stronger sense of your own self-determination: your sense of personal choice and pride in the work you do, knowing that when you sell what you sell and provide the service you provide, it will in some way make life better for your customers.

Let me for the final time remind you that the premise upon which this book is based is: People Get Your Truth. That over time your intentions, promises, actions and results will either promote you as trustworthy or expose you as untrustworthy.

The Building Customer Trust process is a practical blueprint for you that starts with you gaining clarity about your intentions for your customers – a statement of how you want to make their life better in some way. When you start with this mindful intention, you're starting the communication process with your customers based on a genuine desire to earn their trust by promising what you can deliver and delivering on what you promise.

My earlier anecdote about the *Intention-Ometer* suggested that if customers knew the true intentions of the people who were trying to sell to them, they would surely only buy from those whose intentions were to genuinely discover and meet their wants or needs, or solve their problems, or help them to achieve their goals in some way.

By you adopting the Building Customer Trust process, you're providing your customers with an *Intention-Ometer*.

Although the app isn't physically in their hands, it most certainly is in their thoughts and feelings.

Your customers will get your truth; they will get your intention and this is what fast-tracks trust and makes the selling and buying experience a positive one for both you and your customers.

I wish you my very best and would welcome you contacting me on your preferred social media platform or via my davidpenglase.com website.

Acknowledgements

I'VE BEEN BLESSED in both my professional and personal life to have mentors, colleagues, family and friends who have supported my personal mission to make life better in some way for my clients.

This book is the culmination of over two decades academically studying what causes people to think, feel and act the way they do. In particular, my focus for the majority of that time has been around the impact our relationships have on almost every measure of success we use in our professional and personal lives.

I want to thank all of my corporate clients – far too many over the years to list – and I also want to thank the many thousands of sales and customer service leaders and their teams who have engaged and trust me to help them develop the skills, mindset and behavioural strategies to earn, build and maintain customer trust and to enhance their success in winning more new, repeat and referral business.

Being in sales and service roles still often gets a bad rap because of the questionable, unethical and even illegal practices and techniques, often subversively sanctioned by a very small number of leaders of sales and service people.

This book is for all the ethical business leaders and their sales and service teams who genuinely aim to deliver exceptional buying experiences and create high-level customer service.

I'd like to thank my friend Gihan Perera (www.gihanperera.com), who provided such clear guidance throughout a number of versions of this book. A big thanks to my editor, Heather Kelly (www.astorytotell. com.au) and to all the team at Busybird Publishing (www.busybird. com.au) for their professional advice and expertise throughout the publishing process.

I especially want to thank and acknowledge my son Anthony for his advice, assistance and the considerable amount of after-hours work he so willingly provided and continues to provide, in helping me visually represent the many models and graphics that have become such a key part of the Building Customer Trust branding and resources.

And as always, to my wife Liz: thanks for being the backbone of our business, and mostly, just thanks for being you.

About David Penglase

DAVID PENGLASE is a 'hall of fame' international conference speaker, masterclass facilitator, and best-selling author who helps business owners, leaders and their teams achieve more success through building international trust rela-tionships.

Academically, David is a behavioural scientist with degrees in business and the psychology of adult learning. He has an MBA, a Master degree in Professional Ethics and a Master of Science degree in Applied Positive Psychology.

Since establishing his corporate education and conference speaking business in 1994, David has presented his entertaining, energetic and engaging conference presentations to top-tier corporations and associations across Australia and internationally in over 10 countries.

David lives in Sydney, Australia, with his wife and business partner, Liz.

Website:

www.DavidPenglase.com

References

1. Rebecca J. North and William B. Swann, Jr (2009). 'What's Positive About Self-Verification?' In S. J. Lopez and C. R. Snyder (eds), *The Oxford Handbook of Positive Psychology*, 2nd edn, pp. 465–474. New York, Oxford University Press.
2. Anneli Jefferson, Lisa Bortolotti and Bojana Kuzmanovic (2017). 'Unrealistic optimism – Its nature, causes and effects'. *Consciousness and Cognition*, vol. 50/4, pp. 1–2.
3. Chris Anderson (2009). *FREE: The future of a radical price*. New York, Hyperion Books.
4. Vanessa Hall (2009). *The Truth About Trust in Business: How to enrich the bottom line, improve retention, and build valuable relationships for success*. Sydney, Emerald Books.
5. Edelman Trust Barometer: https://www.edelman.com/trust2017/.
6. World Economic Forum: https://www.weforum.org/reports/white-paper-decoding-complexity-trust-industry-perspectives.
7. Stephen M. R. Covey (2008). *The Speed of Trust: The one thing that changes everything*. New York, Free Press.
8. Jan Carlzon (1989). *Moments of Truth: New strategies for today's customer-driven economy*. New York, Ballinger.

9. Carol Dweck (2007). *Mindset: The new psychology of success*. New York, Ballantine Books.
10. Russ Harris (2008). *The Happiness Trap: Stop struggling, start living*. London, Robinson.
11. Neil Thompson (2017). *Existentialism and Social Work*. New York, Routledge.
12. Richard Ryan and Edward Deci (2017). *Self-Determination Theory: Basic psychological needs in motivation, development, and wellness*. New York, The Guildford Press.
13. David Penglase (2016). *The Impact of Good Intentions at Work on Motivation, Meaning and Life Satisfaction*. Dissertation paper UEL MScApp.
14. Joel Barker (1992). *Paradigms: The business of discovering the future*. New York, Harper Business.
15. Paul R. Lawrence and Nitin Nohria (2002). *Driven: How human nature shapes our choices*. San Francisco, Jossey Bass.

Printed in Australia
AUHW011133250220
324216AU00008B/54

9 781925 692396